I0493460

How to Get

Hired

Simple Tips That Work

By

Leslie Le Mon

Copyright 2014, Leslie Le Mon

CONTENTS

"WHY CAN'T I GET HIRED?"

If you're asking that question, you're not alone. *Millions* of people ask themselves that question every day. Millions. And that's part of the answer.

Why can't you get hired? Because even though the economy is gradually improving, there are still *millions* of people out of work. That's a lot of competition in the job-hunting market.

There might be other reasons you haven't been hired, but this is one of the main reasons: There are still *way* too many job hunters, and not enough jobs. It's like a nightmare game of "musical chairs". Every day a few more people get to sit down, but there are still millions of people without chairs.

So when you send out a hundred resumes and applications, and receive only rejections—or stony silence—don't be too hard on yourself. In fact, don't be hard on yourself at all.

Regroup. Take a deep breath. And take heart. Because there *are* simple things you can do to increase your chances of being hired, even in an extremely tough market.

No single book or program can promise you a new job. But this book will improve your chances, and put you in a better frame of mind for job hunting.

Finding a job can be compared to finding a mate. It has to be the right time, the right place, the right match—the right *everything*. There are a thousand little things that factor into the equation, and tip your chances one way or the other. No one can guarantee you a job any more than they can promise to find you true love.

But there are things you might not be doing that will help you find a job. Things that you can start doing today.

And there are things you might be doing that are getting in your way. Things that you should stop doing immediately.

Think of this booklet as a portable job-hunting mentor, a coach, a friend. It will set you straight on a lot of points without any hype or judgments.

Getting hired isn't rocket science, but it demands common sense. Some people seem to have that common sense naturally. Others "learn it and earn it" from experience. If you are a new job hunter, or if you worked for the same organization for a long time, you might not have the benefit of experience to guide you.

How did I "learn and earn" the experiences I share in this booklet? I've been writing resumes and coaching job hunters for almost fifteen years. More importantly, I've been a hiring manager, so I have front-row insights about what goes through the minds of recruiters and hiring managers. And maybe most importantly, I've been a job seeker. I've been through layoffs and long-term unemployment. I've been in *your* shoes, job hunter. That's where a lot of the tips and insights that are going to help you originate.

What are recruiters and managers looking for? How do they *actually* screen candidates? What can get you in the door for an interview (or leave you out on the curb)? How can you avoid wasting time chasing jobs that you probably won't get—and wouldn't like if you did? How can you improve your resume, and sharpen your interview skills? What closes (or sabotages) that coveted job offer? What should you always do, or never do, to land that new job?

This booklet gives you that inside information. These tips are designed to be universally useful. They apply across industries and job types, whether you're a new job hunter or seasoned searcher. The tips are presented in a reasonably logical order, so you can read the book straight through. But this is also a "dipping" book. You can dip into it and read tips randomly; each is designed to be helpful even if read on its own.

Please take a comfortable seat. Open your mind. Prepare for tips and hints and examples and exercises that will give you an edge in your quest to

get hired.

SIMPLE TIPS THAT WORK

#1

BE KIND TO YOURSELF

If you're job hunting, that means you need a job. Which means you might have been laid off, or fired, or widowed, or divorced, or relocated, or lost your business, or experienced some other big life-changing event that's already causing you stress.

Add to that the pressures of job-hunting, and the financial pressures you might experience while you're out of work, and your feelings about yourself might be quite negative at the moment.

After suffering a major life change and starting a job search it's very important that you

Make an effort to be kind to yourself.

You need that kindness, not only for your own well-being, but so that you can project a positive and confident image to potential employers. How you feel about yourself is the foundation of your job hunt, and the foundation of how others will perceive you.

So how can you be kind to yourself—especially when you're out of work and funds are probably limited?

- **Use positive self-talk.** This is especially important when you wake, and before you sleep. We tend to become who we tell ourselves we are. So our internal thoughts matter. Don't criticize yourself. Don't beat yourself up. Use empowering self-talk: *I am not my job. I am a good person. I have value.*

Being jobless is a temporary setback. The right job is out there. I can do this. And so forth.

- **Mourn.** If you lost a job, business, spouse, home—whatever prompted this life-change—*you need to acknowledge the loss and feel the emotions surrounding it before you can move on.* Your mood might change daily—even hourly. You'll experience sadness, anger, frustration, nostalgia, happiness— a whole spectrum of feelings and sensations. Seek professional assistance if needed. Sometimes just acknowledging the loss and feeling the hurt is enough to help you move forward. *The better you feel emotionally and mentally, the better your job hunt will progress*, and the better you will be able to handle the obstacles and disappointments any job search entails.

- **Take breaks.** Don't search twenty-four/seven. Don't become obsessive about it. Build breaks into your search schedule. Take a walk. Catch an inexpensive matinee if you like movies. Listen to your favorite music. Spend time with family and friends. Continue with any hobbies you can afford. These breaks will recharge you; you'll return to the hunt with a clearer mind and more energy.

- **Exercise.** Even a simple daily workout burns off stress, and keeps you healthy and fit. It has also been shown that exercise can life your mood and make you feel better about yourself.

- **Eat well.** When things look dark, it's easy to topple into the black hole of junk food binges. Handfuls of chocolate chip cookies and crunchy, salty snacks are momentarily comforting but can do mid-and-long-term harm to your health and waistline and self esteem. Have that cookie or sundae from time-to-time, but make sure you're eating plenty of veggies, fruits, and protein, and drinking plenty of water. It's not about being thin, it's about being *healthy*. When you're healthy you feel good about yourself and that's what you show the world.

- **Connect with positive people.** Do you know optimistic people who are natural coaches or cheerleaders, people who say or do inspirational things and always leave you feeling upbeat and energized after you spend time with them? *Those are the people you need to connect with right now.* They'll help you keep your energy level up with your eyes on the prize.

- **Tell negative people to go fly a kite.** Well … You might need to be a little more diplomatic, depending on who the negative people are! But as much as possible avoid negative people who always see and expect the worst. If you can't avoid them, tune out their negative conversation as much as you can. People who actively insult you or put you down should be avoided at all costs. (And ask yourself why those people are in your life to begin with.)

- **Reward yourself.** Every time you receive a reply from a potential employer, or get called for an interview, do a little something to celebrate. It should be simple and fun. Take a walk, or pop a chocolate bon-bon (that's one bon-bon, not the box!). Play a happy song and dance along with it. If you have kids and/or a family, get everyone dancing! It's important to celebrate these little victories. Even if they don't lead to a job, they keep you motivated along the sometimes daunting journey.

- **Pamper yourself.** After a day of applications and interviews, pour a glass of wine or beer and relax. Soak in a tub. Zone out in front of a football game, or paint your nails—whatever makes you feel pampered. It's home spa and man cave time!

#2

FIGURE OUT WHO YOU ARE

Do you know who you are? Not necessarily down to the deepest depths of your soul—but generally?

You should. Because when you're looking for a job, *that's what every prospective employer wants to know about you*: Who you are.

What you can do is part of who you are, but it isn't everything. Think about it. Millions of people can write, or type, or paint, or design, or teach, or wait on customers, or sew, or pitch a baseball, or any of a hundred thousand things. Millions of people can do the exact things you can do.

So why should an employer hire *you* instead of millions of other people?

What makes *you* special? What do *you* bring to the table that others don't—or can't?

Part of your job search should be devoted to asking and answering questions about yourself.

This will help you to easily and naturally answer the questions that potential employers will ask you. It will also help you to focus your job search, and ask better questions of potential employers.

Find a quiet place during a time when you won't be interrupted, and ask yourself questions such as these:

- *Do you like fast-paced, steady, or slow environments?*

- *Do you like to work alone or with groups? Or both?*

- *Does it feel more comfortable to follow directions, or give directions?*

- *Do you like to make your own decisions, or collaborate with others to reach consensus?*

- *If you could work anywhere, where would you work?*

- *Where would you intensely dislike to work?*

- *If you could have any job, what would it be?*

- *Would you consider going back to school (whether a bricks-and-mortal school or online program) for additional degrees or certificates if necessary to land a particular job?*

- *Would you be willing to relocate to another city—even another state or country—for a job?*

- *What is most important to you: Feelings, Appearances, Information, or Results?*

- *If you won the lottery, would you still work?*

- *What can you do better than anybody else?*

- *What do you not do well?*

- *Look back at your job history. What led you from job to job? Chart your past course.*

- *Where do you want to be in five years? And what will you need to do to get there?*

As you consider these questions, they will naturally give rise to other questions for you.

These questions are just a starting point. Libraries have many books full of entertaining quizzes and tests that will help you learn more about yourself, your jobs skills and styles, and the types of jobs and industries where you might be happiest. The internet has plenty of those quizzes and tests too.

Being out of work can be stressful, depressing, even frightening. *But it is nevertheless an opportunity.* Being jobless is a pause point where you can look within. Use this chance to learn more about yourself. And use what you learn to communicate who you are to prospective employers, and to find a job you'll love.

Who are you? What do you do better than most other people? What can you offer employers? And what type of job and industry will make you happiest?

Now, when you're job hunting, is the time to ask and answer these questions. This applies whether you're a first-time job hunter or a seasoned veteran. We are all changing, constantly, throughout our lives. Now is the time to get acquainted or reacquainted with who you are.

#3

TELL PEOPLE YOU'RE LOOKING FOR WORK

This is absolutely one of the most important things to do when you begin job hunting, and it is often something people don't do:

Tell people that you are looking for a job.

Why don't people do this?

Sometimes people feel ashamed that they're out-of-work, and are afraid of being stigmatized.

Sometimes it simply doesn't cross their mind how vital it is to get the word out there.

Even if you're feeling depressed or ashamed about being jobless, it's important to spread the word that you're seeking employment. It can be enormously helpful in generating job leads and can help you find a new job much faster.

Think about it: If you, alone, look for a job, that's *one person* trying to find a job for you.

If you tell your friends, families, and acquaintances—even strangers—that you need a job, that means *dozens-to-hundreds of people* are trying to find a job for you!

Studies have been done, and *most people find jobs through other people*. This isn't surprising, given what social creatures humans are.

So if your mother and your uncle and your cousin and your postal carrier and your kids' teachers and your pastor and your manicurist and your mechanic all know you're looking for a job, they *all* have their eyes and ears open. One of them might give you the tip that leads to your new job.

How do you get the word out that you're looking for work? A few tips:

- **Be positive and succinct.** No matter why you're looking for a new job, keep your comments (if any) about your old job *upbeat* and *concise*. No drawn-out, bitter stories of how your boss had it in for you! Simply let people know you're looking for new opportunities and that you'd appreciate hearing about job openings.

- **Let people know what you do and what you're looking for.** If you're a nutritionist and you can only work within the Houston area, let people know that. Be specific. If you simply say you need a job, well-meaning friends and family will overwhelm you with information about jobs for which you are completely unqualified or which are located on the other side of the globe. Save their time and yours. You want to say something like, "I'm a computer programmer and I need a night job in or near Santa Fe." "I do makeup and hair and can work any shift around Studio City or Culver City." "I'm a certified pre-school teacher, and I'll need a job in Portland when I move there next spring." See? Let people know what you do, and where and when you can work. Keep it simple, and you're golden.

- **Use *all* your communication channels.** Reach out to people face-to-face, by telephone, by email, by letter, and via social media tools like Facebook, Twitter, and Instagram. *Everyone everywhere* should know you're looking for that awesome next job. Keep your messages and postings *brief*, *clear*, *positive*, and *professional*.

- **Thank the people who help you.** Even if a job tip doesn't pay off, be sure to thank the person who shared it. Maybe you didn't get that coaching job that Aunt Larissa recommended you for, but she tried to help you. Keep a simple list of your job tips and who provides them and don't forget to say "Thanks".

#4

CLEAN UP YOUR SOCIAL MEDIA

And speaking of social media ...

Now is the time to clean up your websites.

Potential employers now perform internet searches on job candidates. Not *all* employers. But quite a few. Human Resource and recruiting professionals are getting younger and younger. So are hiring managers. They are part of a generation that is connected to the internet and social media twenty-four/seven. When they screen applicants, it's second nature to them to research candidates online.

What will someone find if they Google-search (or Bing-search, or Yahoo-search) *you*?

Will they see photos of you winning "Employee of the Month" awards? Or videos of you throwing a winning touchdown? Will they find your Nobel Prize-winning blog about increasing crop yields to feed the world?

Or will they find ... things that are not so flattering?

I repeat: *Now* is the time to clean up your websites.

- **Start by searching for yourself online.** Use multiple search engines like Google, Bing, and Yahoo.
- **Next, check your own websites (Facebook, Twitter, etc.**).

- **Remove anything you wouldn't want a prospective employer to see or read.** That angry rant about how your favorite basketball team tanked during March Madness? It doesn't exactly make you look like prime employee material. Neither do your snarky comments about a neighbor's barking dog, or that old sorority photo of you passed out at the university tavern. *Anything* that makes you look irresponsible, lazy, unpleasant, immature—*anything* that makes you look bad in *any* way—should be removed or secured by maximum-level privacy settings.

- **If the photo or video or comment you want to remove was posted by someone else (usually a friend, family member, or ex), contact them and ask them to take it down.** Explain that you're job hunting and throw yourself on their mercy. If they're reluctant to remove the item, remind them that photos or videos that *you* took, or words that *you* wrote, are considered copyrighted by *you* under the law. Anyone posting photos, words, etc. that you created is violating your copyright. Crime of the century? No. But they need to remove those items if you tell them to, because you own the items.

- **Photos, videos, or text created by other people—that's trickier.** The copyright belongs to whoever created the materials, so you usually can't make the creator remove the items. However, if the material is particularly damaging, and if the posting of it seems malicious, you might want to consult a lawyer. If your funds are limited, some law offices offer free consultations.

- **Go to your websites (Facebook, Twitter, Instagram, etc.) and set your privacy settings at the maximum level.** This creates a barrier between your online materials and casual searchers—like recruiters—who are looking for information about you. They won't be able to see your site content unless they "Friend" or "Follow" you.

- **Post positive content on publicly viewable sites.** Now that you've cleaned up negative content, it's time to be sure there is *positive content* out there, things that show how intelligent, diligent, and competent you are. Are you looking for a job on Wall Street? Post your thoughts about the stock market, either on your own website or in the comment section of a reputable online stock market publication. Start a blog, even. Are you a photographer? Be sure to post your best photos on a publicly viewable page on your website(s). Posting positive content is important whether you're looking for a job in engineering, education, transportation, or the art world—it doesn't matter what kind of job you want, in what industry. If a potential employer stumbles across engaging and positive material about you online, that can only help your chances of getting interviews and jobs.

If you've finished reading these tips, and you're saying "Huhn? What is Twitter? How do I post things? What are search engines?" then you are not someone who lives online. So you probably haven't posted *anything* about yourself. You haven't posted comments, or uploaded photos or videos.

- **The good news: You haven't put anything on the internet that could hurt your chances of getting a job.**
- **The bad news: Someone else might have posted something that could hurt your chances of getting a job**—but since you

don't spend much (or any) time online, you don't know about it.

- **Consult a friend or family member who is well versed in exploring the internet.** Ask them to help you look for any potentially damaging content out there. Did someone post a video of you tripping over your own feet at the family reunion? Or upload a photo of you with hunks of broccoli caught in your teeth?

- **Ask the people who posted negative or embarrassing items to remove them**—at least for the duration of your job search.

And that's all there is to it, job seeker, whether you're online constantly or are new to the internet. It will take time, and in some cases a bit of negotiation and persuasion, but you *can* clean up your social media and online presence.

Best of all, you can show yourself in a great light by posting positive content.

Wear your passion for your profession and industry on your virtual sleeve! It just might pay off with a new job.

#5

CLEAN UP YOUR ACT

So you're job hunting. You're out of work. There's been some type of big life change that prompted this situation. Maybe you've been laid off, or fired, or have gone through a divorce, or moved to another city or state or country, or suffered a serious loss.

It's understandable that you might let yourself go a little (or even a lot) when you're processing life changes and are between jobs.

Is that really so bad? Will it *really* hurt your chances of finding work if you let yourself go a little bit?

After all, most job searches happen online these days. You're sitting at a computer, filling out applications and uploading resumes. You aren't exactly on the public stage, are you? So does it *really* matter if a job hunter lets their hair go a bit, doesn't shave, and sits around in pajamas at two pm?

OK, sometimes you have to pop into the post office, the library, the job center. But have you seen how people are dressing nowadays? No one seems to comb their hair anymore. And people are walking around wearing their pajamas. Not just to grab the paper off the front porch, or to walk their dog to the corner. People are wearing their pj's to the post office, the grocery store, the library.

So it's all good—right? Letting your hair get a bit shaggy. Not shaving. Dressing like you just rolled out of bed at noon. It doesn't matter, does it?

Well, yes. It matters. In the long run, it absolutely matters.

Let other people walk around wearing pajamas.

You, job seeker, will treat yourself better than that. This links back to Tip #1 "Be Kind to Yourself".

Why does it matter if you let yourself go?

First, because sitting around unshaven in your pj's all day begins to have a mental and emotional effect on you. You're not treating yourself like you have value. And you won't be at your sharpest. It's not about how you look as much as the fact that how you look impacts how you feel about yourself *and* how you project yourself to others.

Second, OK, it *is* about how you look, too. Because you never know when that call or email is going to strike, the one that could lead to that new job. *Try to be ready for an interview at a moment's notice.* Be ready to sparkle.

- **Hair.** Maybe there's not enough coin in your budget for a visit to a Beverly Hills salon, but find a local barber shop or hair dresser with reasonable rates to keep your 'do looking professional.
- **Makeup.** No need for a full face of makeup while surfing the internet job sites, but keep makeup on hand and be ready to apply it when you get called in for an interview or when you visit your local job center.

- **Nails.** If you can't afford a nail salon, be your own manicurist. Inexpensive manicure tools and nail glosses and polishes can be found at nearly any drug store or big box store. Unless you're an artist or entertainer avoid extremely bright, extremely dark, or unusual nail colors. No flowers or psychedelic patterns on the nails—err on the side of conservatism. If you have kids, get them in on the mani-pedi. Make it a fun activity instead of a chore.

- **Wardrobe.** No need to wear a suit or dress while you're at the computer job-hunting, but keep your work clothes in good shape. Have them dry cleaned and store them neatly. Wear them when you visit job centers and prospective employers and when you go on interviews. Organize accessories (ties, scarves, socks, etc.) you plan to pair with each outfit—and hope your teen daughter or son hasn't "borrowed" a key item the day you get the big interview invitation!

- **Shoes.** It makes sense to wear slippers or sneakers while you compose cover letters at home, but keep your professional footwear clean and ready to don when opportunity finally knocks. Always put your best foot forward (literally) at job interviews and when visiting job centers or prospective employers.

- **Grooming.** Treating your job hunt like a job in itself means you're awake at an early hour and that you're washed and showered, as if going into the office. It means you make sure to get enough sleep, drink enough water, and walk or exercise. If the phone rings right this minute, are you ready to pull on your interview outfit and head out the door, feeling good about yourself?

You matter. Treat yourself like you matter. If you don't, the world certainly won't.

Treat yourself like you matter, and you'll be ready at a moment's notice to win that next great job.

#6

CLEAN UP YOUR RESUME

Unless you're a recent graduate or have worked at the same company for twenty years, you probably have a resume. And it's probably out-of-date. It probably doesn't contain any information about your most recent position or company.

If you don't have a resume, you need to write one.

If you do have a resume, you need to update and polish it.

Do you know how to use MS Word, even at a basic level? If so, you can write your own resume.

If not, there are plenty of bricks-and-mortar services and online services willing to write or edit your resume for a fee. Grab the yellow pages (and if you know what *that* expression means, you almost certainly need a resume update) or use an online search engine to find a reputable and reasonable resume service.

What makes a killer resume, a document that will entice employers to contact you for an interview? Remember that a resume is *not* an application. A resume is *not* the place to list every last job you've had or every last job duty you've performed.

A resume is an advertisement—*your* advertisement. In the lingo of Hollywood, it's a highlight reel. Only include the most important information on it, the information relevant to the type of job you're seeking in the type of industry you're targeting. Keep it clear, simple, concise, and positive.

You're the star, and your resume is like your movie poster. Make it engaging. Make it count!

Reading from top-to-bottom, here are some of the key elements of a good resume:

- **What's in a name?** A lot—especially when it's *your* name. Make sure your name is clear and bold at the top of your resume. Don't make it *too* big—that can look vain—but be sure it stands out. Recruiters and hiring managers are inundated with resumes. Don't let yours get lost in the shuffle. Avoid nicknames—particularly cutesy nicknames. Be professional.

- **Contact Info.** Your address, phone number, and email address should appear clearly immediately under or next to your name. Employers will probably correspond with you via phone or email, so why include a mailing address? It shows you have a physical abode, which indicates stability, respectability—all sorts of things—to a potential employer. If you're between residences, use a PO Box, or the address of a trusted friend or family member who will make sure you receive any mail that arrives addressed to you. The phone numbers you include on your resume should be numbers only you (or someone else who's reliable) will answer. And now is as good a time as any to check that your voicemail message sounds professional. "Hey, wassup, talk to me," and similar salutations should be upgraded to a more professional-sounding voicemail prompt. Use an email address that's professional, too. If your current email address is something like "miztercool38" or "littlemisstrouble82" it's high time for a new email handle! Sites like Gmail offer free email addresses. Select a professional-sounding email address that relates to your name. SallyDoe2014, for example. That will impress employers more than "partygrrrl009" or "oldgrump2000"!

- **Summary.** Within the last couple of decades someone came up with the not-so-genius idea for job seekers to post their "Objective" near the top of their resume. The problem is, *most employers don't care what you're objective is.* They haven't met you. They don't know you. Why would they care about your career objective? These recruiters and hiring managers are scrambling to fill open positions and they are overworked and under-staffed and they simply don't have time to care what a stranger's professional objective is. All they can care about is what *you* can do for *them.* So you tell them. In a summary of three or four sentences under your contact information. You clearly state what you do, any degrees you have, any special skills or qualities you could offer them, and your top achievements and places of employment. The summary should include "key words" from the job description. For example, if a job description mentions "detail focus" several times, that's obviously a quality of importance to the employer. You should describe yourself as "highly detailed" or "detail-focused" in the summary. By including a summary at the top of your resume you are making it *fast* and *easy* for recruiters and hiring manager to see that you meet (and hopefully exceed) the job requirements. Could that increase your odds of getting an interview? Absolutely. Here's a summary sample:

Licensed Architect. Residential, Commercial, and Civic. Versatile, detail-focused professional willing to travel or relocate. Notable projects included the Chickapassah Municipal Bridge, Cleveland, OH; the Railey Building (high-rise), Houston, TX; the Vanderberger Estate (private residence), Westchester, NY. M.Arch, University of Chicago. Time Magazine's "Architect of the Year" 2002.

- **Professional Experience.** List the jobs relevant to the job you're seeking. Try to fill any gaps with relevant activities. For example, if you're a house painter and you were out-of-work during 2013, but you wrote a blog about house painting during that time, and did some volunteer work painting a soup kitchen, mention the blog and the volunteer work. Phrase it in a way that makes it meaningful and ties it to your profession and the jobs you're seeking. When writing your Professional Experience, always include *your title, the name and location of your employer, the dates you worked there*, and bullet points that note your *big achievements* and *overall job duties*. Start each bullet with an action verb. Don't list every little thing you did. List the highlights. If you saved your employer millions of dollars or streamlined their systems or reduced waste or sold thousands of dollars worth of product or won awards, highlight those achievements. *What did you achieve, and how?* Express each item in one clear, simple, bulleted sentence. Pedestrian, day-to-day duties can be assumed by the reader or listed in one brief summary sentence. *List only the last ten-to-fifteen years of your professional experience*. Most employers aren't interested in your earlier professional activities, and if you list jobs from twenty, thirty, or forty years ago you're in danger of "aging" yourself out of the running for the job.

- **Education.** List your relevant *degrees, certificates,* and *training.* Include *the name and location of the educational institution.* Include *the degree or certificate or training course title.* Include major *awards* and *honors.* If you attended college, don't list your high school. If you didn't attend college, do list your high school, noting "Diploma" or "Graduated". If you didn't finish high school but did earn a GED, list the high school and instead of "Diploma" or "Graduated" note "GED". *Don't* include your GPA on a resume unless instructed to do so by a prospective employer. Unless you've been asked to include your GPA, including it looks very inexperienced. *Don't* list school activities unless they're extremely impressive and your job experience is limited. In that case you might want to list activities relatable to the job for which you're applying. Don't list your graduation dates; recent dates can make you look young and inexperienced, while older dates can make you seem over-the-hill. In most cases, employers can't *legally* weed out candidates based on age, but employers certainly do read the dates in the "Education" section, and it's difficult to prove that was why you were weeded out.

- **Skills.** If you speak multiple languages or can operate special tools or software or equipment related to your profession in general and this job in particular, this is where you display it. Present the information simply, in grid form if possible. It should read at a glance. No sentences, no paragraphs, no burying the information in extraneous text.

- **Awards.** Did you win a Pulitzer or Nobel Prize—or even a little old "Employee of the Month" award? Note it here if it will help you stand out from the competition. As a general rule, do not include minor awards (like "Good Attendance") unless it somehow relates to something in the job description. Don't list awards that will be confusing to readers or that don't relate to the job for which you're applying. Don't list award dates if those will reveal how young or old you are.

So, those are the basic elements of a solid resume.

How long should your resume be?

Most resumes should be one page per decade, two pages at most. The only exceptions would be CVs (academic resumes that list courses taught, publications, etc. in detail) or resumes for federal jobs, which often have as much or more detail as CVs.

If you graduated from college two years ago and have only had one job, and your resume is two pages long, your resume probably needs to be cut to one page.

On the other hand, if you've been working for thirty years, and had five relevant jobs, and your resume is only one page long, the resume should probably be expanded to one-and-a-half or two pages.

Remember: It's best to go back no further than 10 to 15 years in your "Professional Experience" section.

- **Focus on recent jobs, and jobs where you made major achievements.**
- **Older jobs and jobs where you had fewer achievements should be noted only in passing**. Just list your title, the employer, the location, employment dates, and maybe *a single sentence* summarizing what you did there.

General resume tips:

- Use common, easily readable fonts like Times New Roman or Arial.

- Use 11 or 12-point font for the main text, and slightly larger fonts for headings.

- **Bold** and *italicize* words to make key phrases and sections stand out.

- Proofread, proofread, proofread—spelling and grammar errors can doom your resume to the trash heap.

- Is your resume interesting? Engaging? Have someone you trust read your resume and give you an honest opinion. Is it clear? Will it make someone want to call you?

- The key to effective resume writing and editing is *revision*. You need to constantly revise your resume. Every resume you send out should be slightly different, tailored for each job. Maybe you pull out a job entry that isn't relevant, or add one that is. Maybe you pepper the "Summary" with applicable "key words" that you find repeated in the job description.

Make sure each resume you send is a simple, flattering and informative portrait of you, and that it matches what the employer is looking for.

If you do that, you've already increased your chances of being considered for an interview, and you're closer to landing that new job.

[View a Sample Resume in the "Resources" Section]

#7

PRACTICE YOUR INTERVIEW SKILLS

If you're fresh out of college, you probably haven't been interviewed for anything other than an internship or a job at the campus grill.

Conversely, if you've held the same job for decades, you probably haven't been interviewed for, well, decades. There are likely to be some rust particles and barnacles on your interview skills.

Even if you've been interviewed dozens of times, and are considered by your friends to be the ace of interviewees, well, even then, *anyone* can stand to sharpen their interview skills.

When job candidate finalists are closely matched, that final, extra thing that puts *you* over-the-top, however slight, is worth its weight in gold.

Here are some general tips and exercises for interview preparation and actual interviews:

- **Prep Partners.** Find someone whose feedback you trust and ask them to play the employer role. Don't ask a mom or aunt who thinks everything you do is amazing. Yes, their positive feedback will feel empowering, but you need an honest and measured opinion. Siblings, cousins, best friends, and neighbors often can be brutally honest. If you can afford it, consider hiring an interview coach. If you can't find anyone to take the employer role, you can still role-play your responses. Practice interviewing in a quiet place with minimal distractions. Video your practice sessions and review them afterward. During the review, look for hesitations, weak answers, and weird body language. We all have quirks like touching our noses or constantly clearing our throats. When you see them on video, you become aware of those habits and minimize them during interviews. If someone plays the role of the employer, get their honest feedback after the practice sessions and take notes. How could you improve? As you continue to practice interviewing, select settings that are louder, and have distractions. This will prepare you for real-world interviews in noisy and distracting settings. It happens sometimes. Your interview might take place in a break room that has a loud coffee-maker percolating away, and employees will be popping into the room every other minute getting coffee, opening cupboards, and chatting with each other. If this happens to you, you'll be prepared.

- **Practice Standard Questions.** There are certain questions that most employers ask. Prepare and practice delivering your answers to these questions *ahead of time*, and you will seem much more organized and at ease than interviewees who weren't expecting the questions. **"Where do you see yourself in five (or ten) years?"** You *always* see yourself at the same company. And you *never* see yourself in the boss' seat! **"What's your greatest strength?"** Pick a strength that is relevant to that specific job. **"What's your greatest weakness?"** Beware—it's a trap! Do not share an actual catastrophic weakness. Share something genuine but mild, something that can actually be construed as a strength. *Don't say you work too hard.* That's what nearly every candidate says now.   Pick another weakness that can actually be construed as a strength. And *don't* conclude your answer by saying "Oh, wow—I guess that's actually a strength". *Let the interviewer be the one to say or think it.* Final tip: Never, never, *never* say you don't have any weaknesses. That is one of the worst possible impressions you can make. **"Tell me about yourself."** This request is so huge in scope, so open-ended, that it often throws candidates completely off their game. They go blank, or they start rambling. You, on the other hand, will have a short-and-sweet answer prepared, and you will have practiced it until you can deliver it with casual ease. *Remember, the employer doesn't want to know all about you.* This is not your cue to launch into your autobiography. You should state *where you grew up, where you went to school, the types of jobs you've held,* and *your most recent job.* Throw in *a big achievement or award* that will give you an edge. Did you just win the Academy Award? Were you just selected as the new Dalai Lama? This is the perfect time to mention it. Here's a sample response to the question "Tell me about yourself": "I grew up in Tennessee. Memphis. I attended Nashville State on a football and art scholarship. Then I drew commercial art in New York City. When I was at K&P Advertising I headed the 'Steak 56' campaign—it won the Schumaker Award last year." There it is—that's all the interviewer really cares about when they ask "Tell me about yourself". Where are you from, where'd you go to school, what type of work do you do, where have you done it, and what makes you special? Prepare your answer, practice it, and that's an ace-in-the-hole for you. The best part? You'd be surprised how many times your answers uncover connections between you and the interviewer.

Maybe they—or someone they know—grew up where you grew up, or went to school where you did, or have a similar degree, or worked at the same company. The "Tell me about yourself" question can end up being a question where you really sell yourself to the interviewers and even bond with them.

- **Behavioral Questions.** More and more, HR and recruiting departments and hiring managers are relying on questions that are supposed to be able to predict your behavior in the workplace. In addition to standard questions like "Where do you see yourself in five years?" or "Tell me about yourself," interviewers are asking Behavioral Questions. Sometimes they write the behavioral questions themselves. But often they let a database suggest (even select) questions. There are entire electronic libraries from which interviewers can draw behavioral questions, and custom-design behavioral questionnaires for specific jobs. This is good news for you, because you can assume that most of the behavioral questions you will be asked will be system-generated and follow predictable patterns, for which you can prepare. What the heck are behavioral questions, anyway? They are questions based on the principle that *the way people have behaved in the past predicts the way they'll behave in the future*. Interviewers are likely to ask you to describe a situation at a previous job and explain how you resolved it. The interviewers will pay close attention to your answers, looking for qualities like *resourcefulness*, *honesty*, *ethics*, *problem-solving abilities*, *independence*, *decisiveness*, and *team spirit*, as well as any skills related to the specific job for which you're applying. Take the time to think of real examples from your work history. In past jobs, when did you display *resourcefulness, honesty, ethics, problem-solving ability, independence, decisiveness,* and *team spirit*? Select examples and replay them in your mind. Be ready to describe them in a few sentences. The actual interview questions can be extremely varied, but generally what they are looking for are qualities like those described above. *Your task as the interviewee is to figure out which example from your past will apply to the question.* A question about workplace theft likely has to do with your sense of *honesty* and *ethics.* A question about how you handled something without supervision likely has to do with your *independence* and *resourcefulness* and *problem-solving* abilities. If you are a front-line worker, expect questions where interviewers are seeking an example of how well you *follow directions/rules* and *demonstrate loyalty.* And so on. During your practice interviews and real interviews, be prepared to deliver answers that show you possess the desired qualities. Some common examples: **"Describe a time when you dealt with a difficult customer/client. How did you resolve it?"** Your answer should describe a time when you took initiative, remained polite to the customer/client, followed rules and directions, showed resourcefulness and problems-solving skills, and engaged resources to create a happy conclusion. *Never* describe customers/clients in insulting terms, no matter how difficult they were. Most organizations still subscribe (at least in theory) to the principle that the customer is always right. **"Describe a situation where you found out a colleague was stealing (or doing something else illegal/unethical). How did you handle it?"** This is an *honesty/ethics* question. The answer to this is *always* that you alerted management or otherwise reported the incident. **"Describe a problem you**

encountered at a previous job and how you solved it." Your answer should show *resourcefulness* and *decisiveness* but also that you are a *team player* and engaged others in the solution, and that you *followed rules*. No matter what question is asked, the outcome should be *positive* (you reduced waste, increased sales, saved money, streamlined a process, etc.). Explain *very* briefly what you did and what the result was. Share credit with others who helped with the solution. That demonstrates the *team spirit* companies tend to like. Tailor your answers to the level of job for which you're applying. If you're applying for front-line jobs, expect more questions about being a *team player*, *following rules*, being *honest*, etc. If you're applying for leadership or independent role, expect more questions about *decisiveness*, *independence*, and *problem-solving*. Have answers to these and similar questions ready and practice them *before* you go to an interview. Does behavioral interviewing work? Yes. Just one example: I once interviewed a candidate for a senior administrative position. We asked behavioral questions to see how the applicant handled surprising or difficult situations in the workplace. We wanted to learn if the candidate was resourceful, independent, and able to problem-solve. Well, the answers the candidate gave to almost every question were "I asked my supervisor." "I asked my boss." "My supervisor told me what to do." In other words, the candidate was not ready for a senior role demanding independent thought and problem-solving. The candidate could only function when told exactly what to do and how to handle each situation. Needless to say, we did not hire the candidate for that job. It would have been a terrible match and no one would have been happy.

- **Be On Time.** This cannot be overstated: *Never* be late for an interview. Set seven alarm clocks if you need to. Plan your travel time so that you arrive early, and build in a healthy buffer zone in case of unforeseen delays. There might be heavy traffic, or a traffic accident. Your train might be late. The parking lot you planned to use might be closed. All sorts of delays can crop up. *If you built in extra time, those delays won't make you late.* What's the big deal about being late? It *instantly* puts you on the wrong foot. This is the interview. If you can't be on time for the interview, why would the employer think you could be on time for a regular work day? Yes, there are some employers and interviewers out there who won't care if you're late. But they're few and far between. Some hiring managers are *extremely* serious about punctuality. They'll instantly reject late candidates, seeing the lateness as a sign of disorganization, disrespect—all sorts of negative qualities—and using it as a reason to remove the applicant from the candidate list. Always assume that being late could be a deal-breaker. There are so many applicants for so few jobs. Recruiters and hiring managers are always looking for ways to winnow out candidates. So why would you want to do something—something that was avoidable— that can hurt your chances of being hired? If for some reason you *are* unavoidably late to an interview, apologize *immediately* in a *calm manner* when you arrive. Simply say "I'm so sorry to be late, I know you're busy. I hope we still have time to meet." Period. Don't be over-apologetic. Don't repeat yourself. Don't make excuses, give long-winded explanations, or make a big deal of it. When you do those things, you're just wasting more time! And those behaviors can read as weak. Imagine a company wants to hire an inventory clerk. An applicant arrives seven minutes late. She flies into the room, looking slightly disheveled, and apologizes at length, telling a rather rambling tale of not being able to find a parking space and getting caught in traffic on a one-way street. Is this a good impression to make? Of course not. She's sounding more disorganized, hapless, and helpless by the minute. The interviewers might feel sympathetic to her as a fellow human being. But is this who they want to hire to handle the company's inventory? Absolutely not! What if the candidate had simply entered the room at a calm, dignified pace, smiled, and said "I'm so sorry to be late. I know you're busy. I hope we still have time to meet." There. *That's* the impression you want to make. Polite and collected. A final tip: If you do arrive late for an interview, *don't try to ignore the fact that you're late*. The employer deserves an apology. Make the apology, and then move on. If you're prepared and answer the interview questions well, the interviewers might almost forget you arrived late. But the employer is the one to designate your lateness a non-issue—not you.

- **Be Self-Sufficient.** Interviewers will sometimes ask if you're comfortable in the room where the interview is being conducted, if the chair they ask you to sit in is all right, if the temperature in the room is good, etc. Remember: *Everything is always fine.* Even if the employer has you sitting on a splintery chair in a stifling hot or freezing cold room, *everything is fine*. Similarly, if the interviewers ask if you need anything to eat or drink, you always politely decline. You don't need water or coffee or a bagel. Don't ask anyone to bring you *anything*—even if *they* offered to do so. You don't need to be chomping on a chewy bagel while the interviewer is asking questions. Nor do you need to a cup of coffee sitting at your elbow. What if you spilled it? It can happen. Interviews are nervous situations. Why increase your odds of making a bad impression? If you do bring coffee to the interview, make sure it's in a *securely lidded cup or travel mug*, and place it well away from you during the conversation. Be sure to bring pens and paper to the interview, as well as any documents the employer asked you to bring. What looks more disorganized than a candidate saying "Er, can I borrow a pen?" or "Does anyone have a piece of paper?" Assume you will need something to write with and something to write on during the course of the interview, and bring those materials with you. It's all about looking—and being—prepared and pulled together.

- **Expect to Be Nervous.** *Most candidates are nervous at the beginning of the interview.* That's just how it is. But the good news is this: interviewers expect a few nerves. Recruiters and hiring managers have interviewed dozens, hundreds, even thousands of candidates. They've seen plenty of nervous candidates before. Your nerves are perfectly normal. So get comfortable—or as comfortable as you can—in your chair, and take a deep breath. Your nerves will pass once the interview begins and you start answering and asking questions. Because once the interview gets rolling, one of two things will happen. Either you'll connect with the interviewer and the job, and you'll be so focused you'll forget to be nervous, or you won't connect with the interviewer or the job, and it won't matter to you whether you impress anyone. Either way, the nerves will recede. So stay calm at the beginning, and ride them out.

- **No Fidget, No Freeze.** If your friend or interview coach or video footage reveal that you constantly drum your fingers, clear your throat, tap your foot, or touch your nose during interviews, work on those habits and try to reduce or eliminate them. We all have those quirks, but constant fidgeting makes even the most qualified candidate look ill-at-ease. Conversely, if you freeze and don't move at all, that looks odd and off-putting too. If you tend to freeze during interviews, try to loosen up a bit. During your interview prep sessions, practice making gestures from time-to-time—to emphasize a key statement, for example. Optimal Interview Body Language: Sit up straight in your chair—not like a robot, but like you have good posture. Lean back slightly from time-to-time to project ease. Lean forward slightly from time-to-time to project interest in what an interviewer is saying. Maintain eye contact—don't avert your glance or keep looking down. Don't get *too* comfortable, though. For example, don't lace your fingers behind your head and lean back in your chair—that posture projects arrogance and dominance. For the same reason, don't put your hands on your hips. Avoid closing or clenching your hands, and don't put your hands in your pockets. Folding your arms is a defensive posture—try to avoid it. Keeping your arms un-folded and holding your hands in an open palm position—that's good body language.

- **Listen.** Make a definite effort to listen to what is being said to you. Sometimes when candidates are nervous, they get "balloon-brain". That's the sensation when you feel slightly light-headed, as if your head might float away, and you can't *quite* focus on what's being said. The feeling will pass. Take a breath. Focus. Listen. Let the interviewers finish their sentences before you speak. Don't interrupt or anticipate. Nod and give other non-verbal cues to show that you are listening and comprehending what's being said. If an interviewer says something important that you don't understand, ask a clarifying question. Such questions show that you are paying attention, and that you are confident enough to ask questions—you don't feel the need to "know it all".

- **Be Honest.** Employers often don't spend the time or money to check every application, resume, or interview statement. Employers are pressed for time and money these days—now more than ever. But sometimes, especially when they've narrowed the field to a few candidates, employers *do* spend the time and money to check applications and resumes. *And if you're caught in a lie during an interview, it's curtains for your job chances.* You 100% should not be lying on resumes or applications. And the same holds for interviews. Whatever the interviewer asks you, *tell the truth.* As well as being the *right* thing to do, it's the *smart* thing to do. You might be thinking, "Wait a minute. Tell the truth? Does that mean I should tell the interviewers my last boss was a crook, or that I have ADD, or that I think that interviewer's skirt is hideous?" No. That's not the game plan. You don't start saying every brutally honest thought that pops into your head, the way toddlers do. But the information you volunteer should be true. Don't say you attended Harvard, for example, if you didn't. And you should answer direct questions honestly, polishing them with diplomacy, and giving the minimal necessary information. Here's a fictitious (but very realistic) example: Cliff, a single dad, is interviewing for a security guard job at a warehouse. Cliff's last job was working security at a factory. Because Cliff's son was often sick last year, Cliff missed six days of work to care for the child. The interviewer asks Cliff "How was your attendance when you worked at the factory?" What should Cliff say? What would *you* say, in Cliff's shoes? If Cliff says "I had perfect work attendance," or even "I had great work attendance," those would be lies. On the other hand, if Cliff says "I have a young son, he gets sick all the time, I missed a ton of work to take care of him," that's not exactly going to increase his chances of getting the new job—is it? It's about being honest, but presenting your answer in a way that doesn't destroy your chances of getting the job. A good answer for Cliff to give would be "I had some sick days at the factory. I made sure to call early in the morning so the boss had time to find a temp." It's honest. Cliff had some sick days. But it doesn't go into detail. The sick child isn't mentioned—remember, it's not a prospective employer's business if you have zero kids or twenty, *or* whether they're sick or well. Mainly, Cliff's answer concentrates on *how he handled taking a sick day*. He called the boss early to make sure a temp could be engaged. Cliff showed a consideration for his employer. That becomes the headline of his response instead of how many sick days he took, or why he took them. So be thoughtful about how you answer interview questions. Don't be drawn into talking about health or kids or non-work-related issues. And be diplomatic, but don't, don't, *don't* lie. Don't say you can perform open-heart surgery if you can't. Don't say you have a law degree if you don't. Don't say you studied ballet with the great Nurishkovo if you didn't. Don't pretend to love football just because the interviewer loves football. You see, big or little, lies always lead to trouble. Even if you land the job, a lie discovered later can mean termination.

- **Be Concise.** Don't ramble during the interview. If you're paying attention, you can tell by the interviewers' reactions if you're starting to ramble. Are interviewers looking away from you? Are they glancing at their watches or smart phones? Are their eyes glazing over? Are they making restless movements? If you're seeing body language like any or all of the above, you can bet you've lost them! Try to answer the questions the pose simply and clearly. Give one example per question—a specific example that's to-the-point. Remember, most interviewers ask fairly similar questions. Having practiced different scenarios and examples in advance, you should be able to answer most questions without a lot of thought. Keep it simple and direct. Drive your answers home with concrete details. You didn't' "Reduce rework". You "Reduced it by 50%". You didn't "Save the company a lot of money". You "Saved the company about $25,000." Etc. That's the beauty of preparing and practicing for interviews in advance. You'll have concise answers and details at your fingertips. Many of your competitors won't.

- **Be Professional.** Keep your interview focused on professional, job-related issues. *Don't mention anything personal or potentially controversial.* No religion. No politics. This is *not* the forum to mention that you think the new Pope is doing a great job, or that everyone in the US Senate should be fired! Don't talk about your kids, or grandkids, or elderly parents who need constant care. Potential employers can't *legally* refuse to hire you because you have kids or elderly parents, but *why volunteer the information*? Why even open that door? (An obvious exception would be if you're applying for childcare, eldercare, or healthcare jobs where having cared for children and/or the elderly would be a plus.) During the interview, talk about yourself as a *professional person*. Share your professional history, skills, and achievements. A brief (very brief) chat to break the ice at the beginning of the interview is OK. If you're a Red Sox fan, and you notice a photo of the interviewer standing next to the Red Sox baseball team, it's OK to say "Wow, you met the Red Sox. Terrific!" That's a potential bonding point with your interviewer, so take advantage of it. But aside from moments like that, *focus on the job and why you're a great fit for it.*

- **Be Friendly, But Not Familiar.** Sometimes you really click with an interviewer. It turns out you went to the same school, or play the same sport, or attend the same lodge, or adore shopping at the same stores, or fishing on the same river. Whatever the connection, it's there, and you bond during the interview. Great. That will put you at ease instantly. And human nature being what it is, yes, this connection might increase your chances of getting hired. Recruiters and hiring managers are only human, and human nature dictates that people tend to hire people they like, and to whom they feel connected. *But don't let your connection with the interviewer take you off your guard.* This is still an interview. Now is *not* the time to tell that hilarious story about that night you drank a bottle of peppermint liqueur and had to call in sick to work. Now is *not* the time to reveal you're recovering from a heart attack, or going through a messy divorce. Avoid the pitfall of asking the interviewer personal questions, or acting like you're old friends. Yes, you connected with the interviewer, but you *literally* just met. Don't assume you're going to be best friends and don't assume the job is yours for the taking. Don't say things like "I can't wait to start!" or "Where will my office be?" Stay professional or you could torpedo a promising interview.

- **Be Positive.** Was your last job a nightmare? Would you describe your last boss to friends as an "ape-like pinhead"? Great. You're probably right. But you never, never, *never* say anything like that during an interview. And now you're probably saying "Hold up! What about that section on being honest?" Yes, you should be honest during your interviews. But remember that part about being diplomatic, and about sharing the minimum necessary information? During an interview, it's very important for you to project a *positive* and *optimistic* attitude. That's who employers want to hire— positive, optimistic, can-do people. They don't want to hire people who complain about past jobs and bosses—however right you might be. Are there exceptions? Yes. But err on the side of being positive. If your past jobs come up during the conversation, don't tell a pack of lies, but find a positive spin. *If you have bad job experiences in the past that might come up during interviews, prepare concise, diplomatic comments in advance.* Every job and every boss has *something* good that you can mention. There's always some silver lining, however narrow, to be found. Focus on those positives rather than the negatives. Your last boss was crazy, *but* he wrote a book about accounting. His knowledge and his book—*that's* what you talk about in the interview. Your last job demanded insane hours and everyone there burnt out, *but* they offered an excellent benefits package. The benefits package—*that's* what you talk about in interviews. Take the time to prepare, and you can get through any interview with a positive, can-do attitude that employers will admire, and hopefully want to hire.

- **Be Equitable.** If there are multiple interviewers (and there often are in the final stages of the interview process), odds are that you'll connect with one or two interviewers in particular. Human nature dictates that you'll start giving those interviewers most of your attention and eye contact. Don't. Make sure you're making eye contact with and addressing *everyone* on the interview panel. Don't let anyone feel left out.

- **Be Informed.** Before you go for an interview, research the company and the department and the people you'll be working with if hired. Be prepared to ask the interviewer some intelligent questions—between one and three questions—that show knowledge of the company and the division and the job you'll be doing if you are hired. *Don't* ask about money, vacation days, etc. You might not believe it, but I've had candidates ask me during initial interviews "How many holidays do we get?" Does that sound like a question a real hard-working go-getter asks? Ask company and job-related questions that show you know about the organization and find it interesting. Ask about projects, the company's organizational structure, its mission statement, its charity work, etc. Of course, avoid any embarrassing topics. If the company CEO was just arrested for driving into a lake while on prescription meds, that's a topic to avoid, not ask questions about! Stick to positive subjects. Was the company in the news recently for posting record profits, or sponsoring a charity fun run? Those are the kind of topics you'd want to ask questions about. *Many candidates don't ask the interviewers any questions at all.* So if you ask a couple of smart questions, that could help differentiate you from the other applicants.

- **Be Humble.** Some job seekers mistakenly think that if they rattle off a few brilliant ideas for changing and fixing a company, that will impress the interviewer and land them the job. However, that behavior is often perceived as arrogant. *Most employers want to hire someone who admires the company and who wants to find a way to fit within that company's framework and help advance its success.* Interviewers are not looking for know-it-alls who want to sweep in and start changing things. Even if you are being hired as an organizational expert or change agent, be tactful and cautious in expressing potential changes you might propose. Be sure to express that you admire the company and would like the opportunity to make it even better, *working in concert with the workers and leadership.* There's a lot to learn about an existing operation before changing it. Be confident in your abilities, but be humble and ready to learn when it comes to your knowledge about the company. Don't openly criticize an organization, or describe it as "broken" or "failing". And as mentioned before, stay away from embarrassing topics like company execs getting arrested or departments being audited for financial fraud.

- **Don't Ask About Money During the First Interview.** During the first interview, money is off the table. If wages or salaries were mentioned in the job posting, or if you were able to find a relevant wage/salary range on the company's website (many companies post such information), then you'll have an idea of what the wage/salary range is. If not, you'll have to tough it out until later interviews or the job offer. *Money is usually discussed during final interview stages, when it's down to you and a few other candidates.* In the present economy, many managers and executives have limited latitude when it comes to what they pay. Budgets are planned and approved at least a year in advance, and where budgets are adjusted, they're usually cut, not fattened. So if during the final interview stages, the wage or salary is mentioned, and it's not to your liking, *don't* try to play hardball. Not unless you have other job opportunities lined up. If you'd prefer a higher figure than the one mentioned, diplomatically counter with a reasonable number, but *make it clear the figure they mentioned isn't off the table for you*. The employer will either consider your counter-number, or will explain it's not possible. You can make your decision based on their response, no harm, no foul.

- **Summarize Key Points**. When an interview ends, briefly summarize what you got out of it. That shows the interviewer you were paying attention, that you care about the job, and will remind them of any action items. For example, "Well, it was great to meet you, Sam. What you said about the 'billable hours' project is really interesting, and I look forward to the web link you're going to send me". Keep your summary short and sweet.

- **Provide Resume Copies and Business Cards**. As you leave, present interviewers with a couple of your business cards and an extra copy or two of your resume. This ensures the interviewers have your contact information, and shows forethought, organization, and consideration on your part. However, don't give them large stacks of cards and documents. That's unwieldy and unnecessary. Two or three copies at most are sufficient. And don't press the items on them if they decline. Never press or force *anything* during the interview. Is it a bad sign if the interviewers don't take your business cards and resumes? Maybe. That might indicate they don't expect they'll need to contact you again. On the other hand, maybe you're their top candidate so they already have your contact information at the ready. They don't need extra cards or resumes.

- **Shake hands and smile.** As you say goodbye, shake hands with the interviewer(s) and smile cheerfully. Practice your handshake with friends and family so you have a firm, strong grip. Give one or two quick shakes. Don't overwhelm the person, but don't be timid or weak in your handshake either. A confident handshake and a cheerful smile—those are the final impressions you want to leave.

- **Be Inclusive.** After you leave the interview room, thank the assistant or receptionist (if any) who originally greeted you and showed you into the interview. This might be the person that coordinated the interview session. In the first place, it's good manners to thank this person. In the second place, assistants and receptionists sometimes exert influence of varying degrees. If the finalist candidates are running neck-and-neck, and you made a great impression on the coordinator who is the hub of the office, and whose opinion is trusted, by everyone, *that* could be the tipping point, the thing that puts you over. Offices are intricate, multidimensional ecosystems. Acknowledge—and be polite to—everyone.

Preparing for and then acing an interview involves a lot different factors. This is one of the single most important aspects of job hunting, and should receive a lot of your time and effort.

Put in the work, and you will find yourself getting sharper and better at interviews. Practice interviews *and* real interviews. It's a crucial edge.

#8

FOCUS YOUR JOB SEARCH

Don't apply for every single job under the sun.

It can be tempting to try a broadcast, scatter-shot approach, especially if your funds are tight and you've been out-of-work for awhile. A feeling of desperation can set in. You're ready to apply for anything. Realtors apply to be cops. Astronomers apply to be midwives.

This sort of dramatic stretch doesn't get you anywhere in the long run. If you're a nuclear scientist who can't type, you probably won't be considered for a secretary job. And vice-versa.

Is there any harm in applying for anything and everything? Sure. You're wasting your efforts, which would be better spent on networking and building your skill sets and following up *real* leads.

And if your resume keeps landing on the desk of the same recruiters and hiring managers, *you soon get a reputation as someone who applies for anything*. You won't be taken seriously. You might even be considered a nuisance. Good luck getting called for an interview then!

Think about it. Picture that overworked recruiter or hiring manager, inundated with cover letters and resumes. They're buried under documents and emails. They're drowning. All they want to read are submissions that are at least in the ballpark. Applications from incredibly over-qualified or under-qualified candidates are not welcome— to say the least.

A recruiter picks up a print out and shakes her head. "Oh my gosh—it's that librarian again. Last month it was a janitor position. Then it was the security job. *Now* he's applying for a lab tech position!"

Don't be that person who applies for everything, for jobs that don't match, that don't suit, for which you have no qualifications. That person ends up with a special file—"the round file".

Remember Tip #2, Figure Out Who You Are? This is one area where those results come into play.

Who are you? What are your skills? What is your temperament? What do you know? What are your degrees and certifications? What are your life circumstances?

The answers to these types of questions should be used to guide you toward the best jobs and industries for *you*. *That's* where you network, *that's* where you apply your efforts to get real results.

If you are a shy, analytical person with mathematical skills, a person who prefers a quiet environment, and you can only work days because you have kids to watch at night, why would you apply for a public speaking job that requires you to address groups of hundreds at crowded conventions, and to be away for weeks at a time?

If you can't fulfill the basic qualifications of a job, and it isn't a good match, do not apply for it.

All right. But what about spreading your wings? What about growing and evolving? Trying something new?

Well, that's all to the good. But you still have to be able to fulfill the basic qualifications of any job you apply for.

Consider the example above. A shy mathematician who craves quiet and needs to be at home nights to watch his kids cannot suddenly become a compelling public speaker who attends noisy conventions and is away from his children for weeks at a time. The odds of this transformation working are so minimal as to be nonexistent—unless it's the plot of a movie or novel.

This is a rather exaggerated example, but you take the point.

If you can stretch your wings, if you can push the envelope of your comfort zone and your situation, then go for it. But you cannot fundamentally change who you are or what your obligations are.

You have to search for jobs within a framework of reality.

- Consider what you learned about yourself by completing Tip #2.

- Then take a blank sheet of paper, or open a blank document on your computer.

- Create a document that will help you focus on the types of jobs you realistically can—and should—apply for.

- Take different factors into account. Consider whether you can work nights. Or weekends. Ponder the types of skills you have—or would need to learn and would be willing and able to learn. In which geographical locations can work? Where, if anywhere, could you relocate? Do you need to work alone? As part of a team? Could you be a boss? Could you be a front-line worker? What salary do you need to survive? Do you need a slow or fast pace? Does your place of work need to be on a public transportation route? Etc.

- Take your time. Give this a lot of thought. It's not something to be rushed, because it will be a blueprint to help you organize your job search efforts.

- When your document is finished, review it. What you've typed or written—that's your job search map. *Those are the jobs you're going to go after*. Those that match your skills and needs, and only those.

- There isn't any right or wrong style of job search map. Your document might be a list, or a grid, or a geometric diagram, or something that looks like a spider web. As long as it helps you zero in on the types of jobs you should pursue, the map is doing its job.

- Revisit the job search map periodically and revise it as appropriate if something changes.

Tape the map to your computer or desk lamp or put it on your fridge. Keep it somewhere, anywhere, where it's highly visible and easy for you to consult.

This level of organization and realism will help you from wasting employers' time—and your own.

#9

APPLY FOR DREAM JOBS

Having *just* written in Tip #8 that you should be realistic in your job search, it might seem rather contradictory to tell you to apply for your dream jobs in Tip #9.

To clarify:

Apply for dream jobs for which you're actually qualified and well-suited.

This is where being out-of-work can be a genuine opportunity. It can nudge you to take chances you refrained from taking while there was a steady paycheck rolling in.

Now you have no job—so what do you have to lose? Apply to some of those dream jobs you keep thinking about but never go after!

Scaling Up and Scaling Down

Consider this example: A bartender in a sleepy little Arizona town has always dreamed of moving to Las Vegas, Nevada and bartending at one of the big casinos. Well, heck. He should go for it, if the Vegas casinos are hiring. He should apply. A good bartender in a small Arizona town can be a good bartender at a big casino. The basic skills are already there. The bartender, if hired, would just have to adjust his skills for the larger casino venue.

The example can work in reverse, too. Maybe a Vegas bartender who's been in the game for decades wants to find a sleepy little town and bartend at a tiny, mom-and-pop bar. Fantastic. Why not apply for bartending jobs in sleepy little towns? The bartender, if hired, will just have to scale things down for the smaller venue.

Here's another example: A meteorologist in Western Massachusetts has always dreamed of forecasting the weather at one of the big Boston TV stations. Well, meteorology is meteorology. She'll have to learn the big station protocols, and how to use the more advanced equipment, but she's qualified to do the job. She should apply to the big stations in Boston. Send them a demo video. Network and leverage any connections she has. She's presently out of work, so what does she have to lose? It might be a case of "now or never".

And the same applies in reverse. Picture a famous meteorologist who's ruled New York airwaves for twenty years. Now she might want to ease back, report the weather at a small station in upper-state New York. Wonderful. She can scale it down. She should pursue this dream, if that's what she really wants.

The examples we just discussed involve people who are moving from a smaller to larger venue, or vice-versa, but will be doing basically the same type of job.

When applying for dream jobs, emphasize your *transferable skills*. Your *portable abilities*.

What do you already know how to do that will be important to your new job?

Highlight those transferable skills in your resumes and cover letters, and be sure to mention them during interviews.

I once applied for a high-level analytical job involving much larger quantities and dollar amounts than I had dealt with in the past. I made it to the final candidate phase because I had the core analytical mindset and skills that the job required, and the employer knew I could scale them up to match the scale of the new job.

As one interviewer remarked, "It's just adding zeros. It's just moving the decimal point."

There had been over a hundred applicants. At the end, it was down to two or three of us.

There was a delay of some months in setting the final-final interview, and by that time I had accepted a management position at a major healthcare company. So I bowed out of the interview for the analyst job. I'll never know if I they would have selected me over the competition.

But I was pleased to have made it to that final round, and I did it by showcasing transferable skills and knowledge.

I did it, and you can do it too.

What do you already know how to do that will be important to your new job?

Be prepared to discuss those skills in interview settings, and to give concrete examples.

Drastic Changes

Let's shift gears now.

What about someone who dreams of a career that's *totally different* from what they've been doing?

Now that they're out of work, should they revive their old career dreams, follow the paths not taken? Or is it too late?

The answer will vary from case to case, and will depend on many different factors.

You have to be brutally honest with yourself, and you might want to invite a range of opinions from friends and family members that you trust.

How about a CFO who always wanted to be a singer?

He spent fifteen years overseeing complicated financial transactions at a Fortune 500 company. Recently, he was laid off. Should he follow his dream now?

That depends on one big thing and a lot of smaller things.

The big thing: *Can he sing?*

If he can't sing, or can carry a tune but has *never* pursued singing in the past, the chances are slim to none that he's suddenly going to be able to make a living as a singer.

But if he can sing well, then maybe, just *maybe*, he has a shot.

He should do the exercise outlined in Tip #2. He should complete the job search focus process. He needs a map that can direct him toward singing jobs that he can *realistically* pursue.

Yes. We all know about Susan Boyle. The quiet woman who lived a quiet and obscure life until she took the world by storm revealing her beautiful singing voice on the British "X Factor".

It happened. But she's a rare instance. Boyle is famous largely because her story is so unusual.

The CFO who wants to become a singer should end up with a job map that includes singing at small clubs, weddings, and bar mitzvahs, giving singing lessons to kids, directing a school chorus or music program—you know. The jobs that most real singers end up with. Because almost no one becomes a singing superstar.

Would the CFO be willing to take charge of an elementary school chorus? To direct a high school musical? To give singing lessons? To croon on small stages in small bars, or sing at weddings?

If he's willing to do that, and he can live on the much smaller wages, and if he can handle the unpredictable schedules and the travel and the late hours and the heckling crowds—if his personality and life circumstances and skills allow him to do all that, then he might be able to transition to singing as a full-time career.

He will need to create a new resume listing any singing-related skills and experience he has.

Maybe he sang glee in school, or sang in a band that snagged some decent gigs.

Maybe he was in community theater productions.

Anything relevant and credible needs to be put on the resume.

Then he needs to put together demo videos and portfolios, and get the word out everywhere, especially via social media.

This might sound discouraging. It's not meant to be.

If you were an artist, but you've always been drawn to plumbing, consider it.

Examine your options.

Examine yourself.

Do the research.

Remember:

Apply for dream jobs for which you're actually qualified and well-suited.

Can you do the job? Are you suited to it? Then follow your dream!

#10

WRITE KILLER COVER LETTERS

When you start job hunting, you hear a lot about cover letters.

"Be sure to write a cover letter." "Don't bother writing a cover letter." "Make sure your cover letters are really good." Etc.

What is a cover letter? It's simply the letter that accompanies ("covers") the resume, application, and other materials that you submit to a prospective employer.

Sometimes you'll be printing and then mailing or faxing an actual cover letter.

Other times you'll be saving it and uploading it to a job application website.

Is it worth investing a lot of time and effort in crafting your cover letters? Should you even bother with them at all?

They can be useful if they're well-written and persuasive, and if they land on the desk or computer screen of someone who actually bothers to read them.

Not every recruiter or hiring manager reads cover letters. They don't always have time. If they are screening one hundred applications, and each application has a cover letter, that equals *one hundred extra documents* to read. Whew!

But there are recruiters and managers who read or at least skim cover letters. And in those cases, a cover letter can be a powerful tool to help you move up the candidate list toward an interview.

No cover letter is better than a bad cover letter.

If you dash off a letter and it has spelling errors or grammatical mistakes, the poorly written letter might get you eliminated before anyone looks at your resume or application. Ouch! That smarts! So if you're going to include a cover letter, *make it good.*

There are four general mistakes people tend to make when writing cover letters.

- ***The letters are sloppy, poorly written, and contain errors,*** or
- ***The letters are short and generic,*** or
- ***The letters are long and rambling,*** or
- ***The letter is all about the job-hunter.***

Error Free

It should go without saying that you need to proofread and spell check your letter multiple times. See if a friend or someone else you trust can read it. A second or third pair of eyes will further decrease the chances that the letter contains errors. More than that, does the letter make sense to others? Is it clear? Does it look good?

Don't Be Blah

As previously mentioned, recruiters and hiring managers are swamped. These days, they are often doing the job of other associates who were laid off. Deadlines are tight, and attention spans are necessarily short.

You have to capture the recruiter or hiring manager's attention in *ten-to-thirty seconds* by giving them *just* enough concise and specific information to pique their interest. To make it worth their while for them to review your resume, which in turn could get you added to the interview list.

If you write a brief, boilerplate letter that you copy-and-paste for *every* job application, the reader can sense it.

Dear So-and-so, I am applying for your Senior Librarian position at the Central Library. I have four years experience and a degree in library science. Please call me at your convenience. Sincerely, Earl Blattman.

Not exactly a compelling or scintillating letter. Blah. Yawn. Why should the reader bother to check out Earl's resume or invite him for an interview?

This letter would get Earl put in the "maybe" pile at best.

Don't Ramble and Don't Be All About You

Earl's short, boring letter is no winner. On the other hand, nobody has the time to read a long rambling letter. Recruiters and managers simply won't read it if you make it too long and dense.

Long letters usually go hand-in-hand with the fourth mistake: Making the letter all about the job-hunter. Remember, employers are trying hard to fill positions.

They don't want to read your life history.

They just want to know what would make you a good fit for *their organization*—what you could bring to them.

Crafting An Effective Letter

Study job postings carefully before composing your cover letter. Note any words, phrases, and requirements that seem to be important (they're usually repeated several times) or that could be deal-breakers.

Your cover letter should run about three paragraphs:

- **Paragraph one:** What are your key credentials, what are you applying for, and where did you hear about the job opening. (Where you heard about a job is particularly important if you were referred by someone known to the employer.)
- **Paragraph two:** Brief bullet points outlining your credentials and top achievements, showing what you could do for them, and *matching the key points of their job description.*
- **Paragraph three:** A final killer point, thanks for your time, and please contact me soon.

Bam. Bam. Bam.

The killer cover letter.

A sample:

Dear Mr. Elgin,

I was pleased to learn from Tab Blitzki, your in-house counsel and a Phi Zeta Phi brother of mine at Columbia, that Gibbleman Brothers is seeking a forensic accountant. As a forensic accountant with more than a decade of experience at Watts & Glimere, I am interested in the position.

My credentials include:

- *95% close and 90% recovery rate for Watts & Glimere.*
- *Recovered $10.25M in assets between 2004 and 2014.*
- *Reduced annual investigation expenditures by 50% during tenure as the Director of Forensic Division.*
- *Co-wrote state legislation amending AB892 allowing deep dives into suspect accounts.*
- *Advanced accounting degrees from Columbia, Fordham, and SUNY.*
- *Co-chair, New York State Accounting Society, 2010 – present.*

Gibbleman Brothers has been on my short-list since your Forbes profile in 2010. I would appreciate an opportunity to sit down with you and discuss what I could accomplish for Gibbleman Brothers in a forensic accountant role.

Sincerely ...

Now, I have no doubt someone reading this book is thinking, "Well *of course* this person has a killer cover letter. *They* co-wrote legislation and directed a division and recovered millions of dollars. I didn't go to Columbia. I don't handle millions of dollars. *I* haven't done anything like that."

But the thing is, you have.

Somehow, some way, you've done many things to help the people and companies where you've worked.

It's a matter of thinking about it. Of making lists. And then selecting items related to each job you're applying for.

This cover letter formula applies across job types and industries.

Remember that no matter what your job is, no matter what industry you work in, you have made achievements, and you have accrued some kind of statistics.

Even if official reports weren't run on your work performance, you can make reasonable estimates of your impact on your work environment. At worst, you must have some kind of annual review scores that you could mention.

Let's consider the example of a police officer ready to move up to the detective level:

Dear Captain Biriedo,

I am applying for the Detective position #BH543-1 that was posted on the department website yesterday 05/01/2014. I am a patrol officer with more than four years experience at Division 7, working under Captain Samuelson's command.

My credentials include:

- *Detective Exam: Passed with 89.4% (April 2014).*
- *Sharpshooter Certification (2010 – Present).*
- *84.3% arrest rate with 70.9% convictions.*

- *Experience appearing in criminal and civil court.*
- *Acceptable or Excellent Fitness Reports (2010 – Present).*
- *B.S. in Criminal Psychology.*

Detective Oberland and Captain Samuelson can testify to my long-standing interest in joining the detective squad and my efforts toward that end. I hope you'll give my application your serious consideration.

Sincerely ...

The applicant isn't necessarily a superstar, but she's organized and clear and succinct about her credentials, what she can offer, and her interest in becoming a detective. She also notes credible references who can confirm her abilities and her passion for becoming a detective.

A letter like this usually will get a far more positive response than a generic, boilerplate cover letter or a long, rambling missive where the point of the matter gets lost in all the verbiage.

Of course, the applicant for the detective position will have to meet the basic qualifications. And if there are far more qualified applicants, she might not even get an interview.

But by writing a strong cover letter, she's setting herself apart and increasing her chances of being taken seriously by presenting herself well.

Here's another example. This time the applicant is a waiter. He is someone truly on the front lines of the work force. What can he say, using the cover letter template, to increase his chances of being considered for a waiter job?

Dear Ms. Pergali,

I saw your ad for a waiter posted on the bulletin board at the Sycamore Employment Center, where I am a client. I am an experienced waiter who can work any shift, including weekends.

If you hire me at your Pergali Family Restaurant, you can expect me to:

- *Work well under pressure.*
- *Handle 10 or more stations at a time.*
- *Show up on time and pick up extra shifts as needed.*
- *Build repeat diners for you by giving great service.*
- *Have 0% breakage.*

I work really well with other wait staff and I love serving families and kids, which I know is most of your business. I live within walking distance of the restaurant. Please call me if you would like me to come in for an interview.

Sincerely ...

This is a great letter because it's simple but it took a lot of work for the applicant to put it together. A lot of thought went into it—and a lot of thought should go into *your* cover letters.

The writer hits all the key notes. Where did he hear about the job? What could he bring to the job? He might not have saved his past employers millions of dollars or won fancy awards, but he can handle heavy workloads, is flexible about his shifts, likes the customer base for this particular restaurant (families and kids), lives near the work site, and doesn't break dishes. These are all great selling points.

By now you can see a pattern emerging. To write the killer cover letter, do your homework. Know what the employer is looking for. Know how you can deliver what they need.

Then craft a simple letter that makes it clear why *you are what they're looking for.*

It doesn't have to be Shakespeare. It just has to be brief, clear, and effective.

#11

SAY "THANK YOU"

Parents teach kids to say "Please" and "Thank You". It's a lesson that tends to stay with us our whole lives.

"Please" and "Thank You" are important tools in your job search.

The applications, cover letters, resumes, and portfolios you send to prospective employers are the "Please". As in, "Please hire me. I'll be *awesome!*"

So what about the "Thank You"?

Many job hunters think they should say "Thank You" after they receive a job offer.

But the first official "Thank You" should be said much sooner— after an interview.

Like every other tool in your job-hunting kit, the "Thank You" should be short, engaging, and to-the-point. And it needs to feel sincere.

Why do you send a "Thank You" message to an interviewer?

If you want that job.

If you're sitting in the interview thinking "Wow—I really want this job!" then you should be taking notes of things that are working during the interview, points where you're agreeing with the interviewers, etc. You can weave those into your subsequent "Thank You" note.

On the other hand, if you realize during an interview that this job is *not* for you—maybe you realize you don't have the skills for it, or that the pay is 25% of what you anticipated and not enough to live on, or that the manager shouts and curses at her staff, or that it will be a five-hour commute each way, every day—if for *any* reason the job is not for you, don't bother to send a "Thank You" note. *"Thank You" messages signal interest.* So if you're not interested, let it go.

How should you express your thankfulness to your prospective employer?

- **A simple message will suffice.**

- **Don't send gifts or flowers, even if that seems like a good idea in the moment.** Maybe you and the interviewer went to the same college. It might seem clever to send her a cap or T shirt emblazoned with the logo of your dear old alma mater. If the interviewer mentions he likes to garden, you might be tempted to send him seeds or plants. If the interviewer has a big bowl of candy on his desk, and mentions he's addicted to chocolate you might be tempted to send a box of chocolate creams to the office. Does the interviewer decorate her office with baseball memorabilia? You might think it's a grand idea to send her a couple of tickets to the next big game. So, kudos to you for being observant and wanting to go the extra mile. *But sending a gift to interviewers, whether it's a tiny gift or an elaborate gift, is not a good idea.* Gifts can seem like attempted bribes. Or like you're trying too hard. Even like you're desperate—and remember, desperation is a job-repellant. Your gift can even be misunderstood as a signal that you want to ask the interviewer on a date. For all of these reasons, don't send gifts.

- **Don't telephone to say "Thank You".** Unless you made an *incredible* connection with the interviewer, avoid calling them to say "thanks". They're busy. They're already answering plenty of business phone calls in any given day. Adding another call to their workload just to say "Thank You" could be an irritant.

- **Do send an email or an actual note.** Send your "Thank You" message two or three days after the interview. That keeps you fresh in the employer's mind, without being over-eager.

- **Use either email or a simple note card or slip of paper.** Stick to pale, plain backgrounds—white, cream, dove-grey, etc. Avoid cartoons, giant logos, wild designs, etc. Nothing unprofessional or distracting. This is a professional "Thank You" note, not an invitation to your next awesome kegger-BBQ. One exception to the "keep it plain" rule would be if you're applying for a job in a creative industry. Are you an artist, photographer, actor, or singer? If so, a brightly colored paper with some type of design might be appropriate. But even then keep it relatively conservative and *make sure your words don't get lost in the design.*

- **If your handwriting or printing is clear and legible, consider manually writing the "Thank You" note.** *Hand-written messages are increasingly rare* and show an extra effort that just might help nudge you over the top if you're in close competition with similarly qualified candidates.

- **Address the message to the person who interviewed you.** If multiple people interviewed you (e.g., a panel), address it to the person who ran the interview. (*Make sure you know that person's name, title and email address before you leave the interview.*)

- **Be brief.**

- **Anatomy of a "Thank You" note:** Include *your name*, the *position* for which you interviewed, and the *interview date*. Remember that recruiters and hiring managers are often filling multiple positions simultaneously, and they interview numerous candidates. Make sure they know who you are and what job you applied for. *Thank them for their time.* Mention *one or two specific points where the interview went well*, and that highlighted why *you* would be a great hire. After all, that's the main point of the "Thank You"—not only to thank the prospective employers for their time, but to reiterate why *you're* the best hire. Then *sign the letter* and *include your current contact information.*

A sample:

> *Dear Superintendant Yu,*
>
> *A quick note of thanks for the Master Electrician interview on Monday. I appreciate your taking the time to meet with me about the open position at Rodriguez Middle School in mid-town.*
>
> *As we discussed, my years of experience as Head Electrician at Garvey Elementary and Garvey Middle School will let me hit the ground running at your school. And the rewiring project in your auditorium sounds like a challenge I would really enjoy, since I handled similar projects at several other schools in the past.*
>
> *Please call me if you have follow-up questions. I look forward to hearing from you.*
>
> *Sincerely ...*

- **Your "Thank You" letter should sound professional.** Even if you bonded closely during the interview, don't send the interviewer a casual "Thank You" message; "Yo, man, what up?" is not the proper salutation (!)

- **Still, your "Thank You" should have a friendly, comfortable tone.** Reinforce the connection formed during the interview. Avoid slang and overly casual phrases, but don't be as formal as you were in your cover letter and resume.

Another example:

> *Dear Mrs. Angelino,*
>
> *Thank you for meeting with me Thursday. I enjoyed learning more about your Construction Manager position, and I was glad to have the chance to tell you more about my experience in Boston and Philadelphia, especially working on "The Big Dig" and supervising construction of One Benjamin Place.*
>
> *I agree with your thoughts on scalability. With my background in small <u>and</u> large-scale projects, I know could be effective managing your company's many different projects.*
>
> *Please call me with any questions. I am very interested in this job and look forward to hearing from you.*
>
> *Sincerely ...*

- **When you close the letter, avoid phrases like "Call any time" or "I'll be waiting for your call"**—anything that sounds passive or desperate, like a tween waiting by the phone for a cute classmate to call. *Keep it cool.* You want the job, but you don't want to sound like you're hanging on by your fingernails, even if you are.

- **Don't be afraid to say you want the job. If you want it, say it.** Especially if you have strong qualifications. *Employers sometimes write off highly qualified candidates if they aren't sure the candidate really wants the position.* Be clear that you're interested. Say it at the end of the interview, and then use the "Thank You" note as a forum to reiterate your interest.

- **Should you address the recipient by their first name in the letter?** Yes, if the interview went very well and you were on a first-name basis with them by interview's end. Yes, if you're applying to a casual or "young" company where everyone is on a first-name basis and using a surname would seem stuffy.

- **Let it flow.** A lot of care and time goes into crafting a "Thank You" note, but when you're finished and you proof-read it, it should sound like you dashed it off: An easy read with a couple of positive points about your qualifications.

Now it's time to hit "Send" or drop the note in the mail.

You've just given yourself another edge in your quest to get hired!

#12

SEARCH HIGH & LOW

People often limit their job search without meaning to do so.

Where and how are you searching for job opportunities?

- Older job hunters might read the newspaper classifieds, bulletin boards at employment agencies, job centers, libraries, and schools, they might cold call businesses in the yellow pages, and attend job fairs—the classic, old school, paper/phone/face-to-face approaches.

- Younger job hunters might search exclusively online, via online job search engines and websites and social media. That's the typical approach in the digital age.

Neither of these approaches is all right or all wrong.

The best approach is a combination.

You want to search high and low, everywhere, using old school *and* new school tactics. Leave no stone unturned.

Upgrade Your Tech Knowledge and Skills

Job hunters who aren't comfortable with technology should dedicate some time during their job search to becoming more comfortable with technology. *Most jobs today require some sort of familiarity with technology, however simple.* If you are tech-phobic, *that might be restricting your job search* and *it might limit your job offers.*

- **You don't have to become a tech guru, but learn the basics.**

- **Consult a child, grandchild or young neighbor who can tutor you** in the basics of email, texting, job search engines and alerts, smart phones, and social media. This can be a real opportunity to let your kids or grandkids share knowledge with you, paying you back for everything you taught them over the years. It can be a fun experience.

- **Or you can take a free or inexpensive class.** Many are offered at local libraries and schools, and specifically target people who feel uncomfortable with new technology but need or want to learn it. Help is out there if you look.

Classic Tactics

Younger job hunters might want to consult parents, grandparents, or older neighbors about the fine art of cold calls, written correspondence, and face-to-face conversation and persuasion.

- **Texting and smart phones only take you so far.** The human connection is always what wins the day.

- **Do you feel comfortable chatting with strangers** (whether in person or on the phone) about whether or not they have a job opening?

- **Do you have an "elevator speech"**—a spiel of less than a minute that will "sell" your skills to someone you just met?

- **Can you write a persuasive letter**—not a text message, but actual formal, professional piece of correspondence?

Those are all skills that many older people learned years ago, in the ancient times that predated smart phones. And if you ask politely, many older people will be happy to share their skills with you!

A Happy Medium

Middle-aged job hunters tend to have an edge when it comes to job hunting tactics.

People who are in their late 30's, their 40's, or their early 50's straddle the analog and digital eras. These job seekers tend to be equally at home whether reading job postings thumb-tacked to job center bulletin boards, or searching for jobs on the internet.

That's the way to search. Use every possible tool and method you can think of.

You could learn about your amazing next job *anywhere*.

#13

STRUCTURE YOUR SEARCH TIME

You've heard it before, no doubt: Searching for a job *is* a job. A full-time job.

So structure it like a job.

- **Full Time Job.** Devote four or five days a week to the search.

- **Regular Schedule.** Pick a time to get started, a general meal time, and a time to quit for the day. If you're an early bird, you might get started at 6 am and stop for the day by 3 or 4 pm. If you're a night owl, you might get started and end later in the day.

- **Office Space.** Set up a place in your apartment or home where you conduct your online searches. It can be very simple. Organize it like a home office, with pens, pencils, paper, paperclips, stapler, your computer, phone, and, if you have one, a printer/scanner/fax. Use inexpensive, clearly labeled folders to organize the documents for your applications, one folder per position. Alpha-sort the folders by company name and position; that will make it easy to find the right job folder if you get a response weeks or even months after you submitted your application. If music helps to inspire you, set up a radio or iPod dock in this space, and play the music that keeps your job search momentum going.

- **Do Not Disturb.** Tell other people who live with you that you need to be undisturbed for "x" hours during the day. (Unless, of course, it's an emergency.)

- **Get Out of the Office.** Schedule some days as "field" days. That's when you go to the library, the employment office, and other places where you can search for jobs. Those can also be days when you visit businesses that might want to hire you, giving them your resume and business card, and—if you're lucky—talking to someone in HR or recruiting.

- **Be Professional.** Try to avoid personal calls and emails during your job search hours, as well as spending time on Facebook or the internet if it doesn't pertain to job hunting. Be available for any employers that might want to converse with you.

- **Child's Play.** If you have kids, and can't afford child-care, which is quite common after a job loss, you might be caring for your children while conducting your job search. That can be a juggle. It's a real challenge. *But you can do this.* Infants and toddlers have nap times. Even when they're awake, you can occupy them with jumpers, toys, mobiles, and games that they can play independently within your line of sight. If you have an active toddler who is always on the move, trying to climb the furniture and see what happens when they pull apart the appliances, then, yes—that is going to impact your job search. If you have to watch and interact with your child almost constantly, you will not get much job hunting done. See if there is a relative or friend whom you trust and who's good with children who can sit with the child in your house for a few hours each day while you job search. As far as older children, they spend a large part of the day at school. You can organize your job search schedule around the school drop-off and pick-up times. Remember too that while you do need to job hunt, *extra time with your children can be wonderful*. Take breaks to enjoy their company now, before you're working full-time again.

These are suggestions that you might find helpful, but you know yourself best. You might work better with less structure. But *some type of structure will make your search more efficient*, and give you that *sense of purpose and accomplishment* that is so important in keeping a positive spirit during challenging times.

There will be discouraging days. Remember Tip # "Be Kind To Yourself". Give yourself a break to clear your head if you need it. Don't burn out.

Then get back on the computer, back on the phone, head out to the employment office.

Finding a job is your job, and you can do it.

#14

TAKE ON PROJECTS AND VOLUNTEER

There are many obvious disadvantages to being out of work, but here's one most people don't think about:

As soon as you stop working, you enter a zone of career "dead time".

People who are working continue to ring up sales, rack up statistics, achieve milestones, win awards, and take professional training that keeps them up-to-date in their industry.

You? You're pounding the pavement, trying to find a job. You're on the phone and computer, trying really, *really* hard not to give in and eat that pint of cookie-dough ice cream in the freezer!

Many employers are wary of hiring people who've been unemployed for awhile, because of career "dead time". They figure you've gone soft, professionally speaking, that you're behind when it comes to current knowledge and skills in your field.

You have to show prospective employers that while you were out of work you were staying current and keeping busy in your field.

Luckily, you have the time to do that. Part of your job search should involve keeping up-to-date with your industry and being productive in your area of expertise. OK, no one has hired you yet—but there are other ways to stay productive besides working a full-time job.

So if you gave in and picked up that pint of cookie-dough ice cream, please put down the spoon. You can do this!

Say "hello" to *projects* and *volunteer work*.

Working on projects and/or volunteering in your industry serves multiple purposes.

First, it keeps you busy, sane, and useful. This is important for morale, attitude, and psychological health.

Second, it generates items for your updated resume and cover letters.

Third, it gives you killer answers for interview discussions. When you go on a job interview, employers might ask "What have you been doing since you were laid off?" What do you say?

- "Nothing." "Job hunting." "Watching daytime TV. Can you *believe* Lance cheated on Kennedy?" "Crushing level 1,000 of 'Candy Crush'!" None of these are good answers. None of them will get you hired!

- "Painting the local library." "Planning the annual church picnic." "Coaching neighborhood Little League." "Keeping books for the local Senior Center." "Designing websites." *These are all much better answers.* These answers might give you a shot at being hired. You've been productive during your time out of work.

Whether you're a mechanic, plumber, coach, accountant, writer, athlete, decorator, web designer, event planner—whatever you do, *someone needs your skills, expertise, and encouragement.* So go for it.

Help others, and help yourself. *Just be sure to pick a project or volunteer activity that relates to your job field.*

Fourth, volunteering and working on projects keeps your skills and knowledge current.

Consider this example. A carpenter who's out of work volunteers to help build an addition to a local civic building. Maybe she gets paid a little bit, or maybe she helps for free. What are the benefits?

- **Networking.** She's working with other carpenters and contractors.

- **Up-to-date Equipment and Knowledge.** She has the chance to use current tools and equipment, and to exchange building ideas and strategies with her peers.

- **Receiving Knowledge.** She can be mentored by more seasoned carpenters—a volunteer job becomes a master class in carpentry.

- **Sharing Knowledge.** She can mentor less experienced peers. She is training them.

- **References.** If she does well on the project, the site boss might write a job recommendation or serve as a job reference. Every reference and contact helps.

- **Job Opportunities.** Finally, if her peers at the job site know of a long-term project or permanent job for which she might be qualified, they'll tell her. *Projects and volunteering lead to networking and long-term or permanent jobs.*

Note that if you're presently collecting unemployment, there are strict rules about *how much you can earn* and *under what circumstances.*

Consult your local unemployment website or call or visit your local unemployment office for details.

Depending on the unemployment rules that affect you, consider taking on projects *pro bono*—for free, for the greater good—or at an extremely reduced rate.

After all, the benefits you *really* want to reap are the priceless experience of helping others, networking, learning, and filling in those gaps on your resume.

#15

GET SCHOOLED

Another good use of your job search time is to study.

Remember Tip #2 "Figure Out Who You Are?"

> **What is it that you don't know that you'd like to know? What is it that you can't do that you'd like to do?**

Try to link your learning to knowledge or skills that will help you get hired.

- When you review job postings, are there requirements that you can't meet because there's something you don't know or something you can't do?

- When you go to interviews, are the employers mentioning knowledge or skills that you don't have—and could *that* be what's keeping you from closing the deal and landing the job?

Many years ago I had two interviews at a Los Angeles Public Television station. The position was being the administrative "right arm" for one of the directors, helping to keep her organized.

The HR interview went very well, and the subsequent interview with the director went very well.

So the job seemed like it was just within reach … but I didn't get it.

Why didn't I get it? What was the stumbling block? It was clear when I compared my skills and qualifications with the job requirements. The station preferred that the person assisting the director know MS Word, Excel, and PowerPoint. But at that time, I didn't.

During the interviews I had told the HR rep and the director that I was a quick study, and based on my background and credentials, they believed me. Sure, I could probably learn Word, Excel, and PowerPoint on the job … But *if someone with similar qualifications already knows that software*, why should the station wait for me to catch up?

That's what you will find during your job search if you are competing with candidates who are similarly qualified to you. *The candidate who already has the knowledge and skills will get the offer.* So you want to be that candidate! Few applicants will have every single skill and ability that the employers want. But *you want to be the candidate who has most of them*—more than your competitors do.

Needless to say, after realizing I'd lost out on the Public Television job because I didn't know MS Word, Excel, and PowerPoint, I ended up enrolling in a free training program through my job center. I became certified in Word, Excel, and PowerPoint (software that was then very new), and because of the training I landed a new job *before* I even graduated from the program.

The right knowledge, the right skills—those are powerful tools. Especially in this job market. You can be smart, you can be hard-working, you can have a solid job record, but you have to have current knowledge and skills too.

It's time to get schooled!

- **First, identify *what* you need to learn.** Do you have to learn a software program? A method of accounting? How to use a particular type of saw or drill? A foreign language? Do you need to brush up on your grammar or spelling? Some engineers, for example, have fairly atrocious spelling because they're focused on numbers and physics. If they worked at the same aerospace company for twenty years, coworkers just accepted the engineers' bad spelling, because the engineers' work product was otherwise top-notch. But now the engineers are job hunting, and other companies are sticklers for proper spelling. Time for the engineers to brush up on rules like "i before e, except after c"! Are you a supervisor, manager, or executive? If so, are you current on your leadership skills, your project management techniques, your knowledge of hiring, discipline, motivation, and how to handle harassment allegations and hostile workplaces? *Don't fall behind while you're job hunting.* Take classes to maintain your knowledge and edge, as well as filling in any gaps you discover.

- **Once you know *what* you need to learn, consider *how* to fill your skills or knowledge gap.** What are the best ways for you to study what you need to learn? Most likely you'll need to combine several different learning methods.

Online Learning

We live in a golden age of just-in-time learning. You can look up almost any subject online and find free guides, manuals, and tutorials so that you can become proficient in it. The beauty of studying online is that you can set your own pace and schedule. There used to be a stigma against online learning, but this stigma has largely disappeared. Even top institutions offer online or distance-learning classes and programs now.

Classroom Learning

Online education is great, but there are still plenty of old-school ways to learn. There are adult classes offered through your local unemployment agency, job center, library, schools, and senior centers. These classes are often inexpensive or even free.

Self-Directed Learning

And then there's your local library, where you can check out books and DVDs that teach all manner of skills. Read, view, and study them at your own pace.

Tutors/Mentors

Some people learn best from a tutor or mentor. And if you're out of work, some mentors will charge a purely nominal fee for the subject(s) you need to master.

Certificate and Degree Programs

In some cases, you'll need to earn a certificate or degree or get your license in a particular area.

Degree, certificate, and license programs, whether held in a classroom or online, *often involve some type of cost*. If your bank account has been hit hard during your unemployment, talk with the school about financial aid or payment plans.

- **Avoid committing to spending thousands and thousands of dollars that you don't have,** especially if the program involves a major shift in your career direction. There are a lot of reputable schools and learning institutions out there, but there are some questionable (and very expensive) places too.

- **Think carefully before you make a big career change** (and spend thousands and thousands of dollars to do it!). Is this really a career that you will be good at, and that will suit you? For example, there are many ads for culinary schools on television these days. In the ads it looks like everyone is having a fun time cooking, and the commercials imply that once students graduate, they'll be running their own restaurant in no time! Having spent many early years in food service environments, I can promise you that working in a kitchen is a busy, sweaty, high-pressure experience. They don't show *that* in the commercials! You *really* have to want to work in that environment. Even chefs—especially chefs—are under tremendous pressures and work long, long hours. If the culinary world is your dream, it can be rewarding, and worth going through the (sometimes expensive) training process. But it's not something to do on a whim. Is this really where you see yourself in five or ten years?

- **Research the learning institution. Thoroughly.** There are a lot of ads for technical colleges out there, too. Are these technical schools reputable? Can you really earn your degree in less than two years? Can they really place you in a good-paying job after you graduate? Many of these technical and trade colleges sprang up with one goal—to make money. Yes, some of them are legitimate, but some are "student mills". The school wants to enroll (and bill) as many students as possible, so *the school glamorizes the careers for which it offers certificates and degrees*, and *it glamorizes what your life will be like after you graduate*. Before you enroll in *any* school or college, research the institution. Is it accredited? Have there been credible complaints filed against it? There are always complainers, everywhere, but if you find a lot of complaints against a school, and the complaints seem to follow a pattern, there is probably some real fire fueling that smoke. What about price? Is the school charging reasonable tuition and fees? Is the expense comparable to similar institutions? Does the school offer financial aid?

- **Ask hard questions.** You have every right to ask a school's recruiter or admissions office questions about the schools' credentials, its job placement rates, how many job openings are *really* out there in the job market, realistic salary expectations, burnout levels in the field, and so forth. *If you're going to be paying a school good money to train and educate you, make sure it's for something you'll really want to do, and that there will realistically be a job out there for you once your learning is complete.* No school can guarantee you a job, but there should be a realistic shot for you to find one. Notice how the school responds to your questions. Do staff members seem uneasy with your questions, or resentful? Do they give you straight answers, or are they vague and evasive? *Any reputable school is happy to answer questions for prospective students and provide concrete data and statistics.*

Trade Publications

In addition to learning skills that will help you get hired, you should try to keep up with your industry. If you can't afford a subscription to the newsletters, magazines, and trade papers in your field, you can find a lot of that information online, for free.

Professional Organizations

If you can afford the membership fees, join organizations where you can interact with your peers and share ideas and knowledge.

Many professional organizations offer lectures and classes that are either free or relatively inexpensive. Attending them will help to keep you educated and informed about your industry. And meeting with your peers will lead to an exchange of knowledge and, quite possibly, job leads.

Now, let's put it all together.

Once you've acquired your new knowledge and skills, add them immediately to your resume or CV and mention them in your cover letters and during interviews.

To sum it up:

- **Find the Gaps.** When you read job descriptions and attend interviews, figure out where you are missing skills and knowledge that you need to be hired.
- **Fill the Gaps.** Then find the best ways to acquire those skills and that knowledge. It will probably be a combination of online, printed, and face-to-face learning.
- **Save Money.** Explore free and inexpensive options if you're on a tight budget.
- **Be Flexible.** Consider studying for a new career if there are few-to-no job openings for your current expertise.
- **Be Skeptical.** Research, very carefully, any learning institution you plan to attend, especially if it will involve a large investment of money and/or time. Is the school reputable? Will earning a degree or certificate there increase your chances of finding a job?

- **Read and Join.** Trade publications and professional groups can be as educational, sometimes, as a formal class or school program.

- **Show.** Add your new skills/knowledge to your resume or CV, and to your cover letters.

- **Tell.** Mention your new skills/knowledge during interviews.

Congratulations! You've given yourself an important edge in the job market!

#16

CREATE A JOB

It happens to most job seekers, especially if they've been searching for awhile and aren't getting any response. They begin to feel discouraged.

You've done everything right—but employers *still* aren't hiring you. Maybe they aren't even calling you for interviews.

What's going on? Why aren't you getting hired? There are a number of possibilities.

- **It might be that you are competing with thousands, even millions, of other job seekers who have similar credentials.** This happens when government agencies, or schools, or manufacturers have mass layoffs. Suddenly there are thousands of teachers competing with each other, thousands of data analysts applying for the same few jobs, thousands of engineers throwing their hats in the ring for one or two open positions.

- **Possible Solution:** *Networking.* Try to make sure someone in recruiting/hiring at a prospective employer is waiting for your application. Leverage your connections.

- **It might be that your job is pretty much obsolete now.** If you are an expert in 17th-century tapestries, or a cuckoo-clock builder, or an ichthyologist (that's an expert on fish), your job opportunities might be *very* few and far between.

- **Possible Solution:** *Relocating* or *Changing Careers.* Whether you relocate, or go back to school, it's going to be a big change and a big investment. Do your research and think it over before making any drastic moves.

- **It might be that you're a renaissance person.** You can do a lot of things very well. That's admirable—but *prospective employers don't always know how to classify an applicant who is multi-faceted.* Employers tend to look for carpet cleaners who have always cleaned carpets, librarians who have always worked in a library, glass blowers who have always worked with glass—and so on. If you're a seamstress *and* violinist *and* computer programmer, employers don't know how to classify you—so your application and resume might end up in the "circular file" (that's the trash can).

- **Possible Solution:** *Rewrite Your Resume.* Each employer should receive a copy of your resume that focuses on the skills and job experience that will appeal to them and their industry, downplaying skills and jobs that are less relevant.

- **It might be that no one is hiring in your region right now.** Especially if you live in a small community or sparsely populated region, there are very few job opportunities that open up each year.

- **Possible Solution:** *Relocating or Changing Careers.* As noted above, do your due diligence and soul searching before making dramatic changes to your life.

- **It might be that plenty of companies are hiring, but you live in a highly populated area.** Astronomical numbers of applicants compete for every job in densely populated areas.

If you live in or around cities like Boston, New York, Atlanta, or Los Angeles, It's hard to stand out in crowds that large.

- **Possible Solution: *Networking.*** Make sure someone in HR or recruiting, or even the hiring manager, is expecting your application and resume. Leverage your connections through your job search boards, professional groups, school, past jobs, former bosses, etc., and *always* be on the lookout for new connections.

The possible solutions offered above can work in the right circumstances. And since you know yourself better than anyone else does, you can probably think of other solutions tailored to your specific situation.

But here's an "out of the box" idea: *Create your own job!*

Mind the Gaps

Every day you interact with the world. You wake up, brush your teeth, get the kids dressed, put out the trash, drop the kids at school, run errands, mail letters, use your computer, shop for groceries, pay your utility bills, catch a movie, grab a salad—you get the idea.

And almost everywhere you go you find *service gaps* and *knowledge gaps.*

You probably aren't even aware you're noticing them. Except when a service gap or knowledge gap *really* annoys you—enough for you to rant about it to a friend or spouse!

"I stood in line for twenty minutes at the post office. Twenty minutes! Just to buy stamps!"

"They only had *two* registers open at the drug store—again!"

"That bank teller was so rude to me! They're *always* rude at First National."

"Have you passed the gas station lately? It looks like it's going to fall down any second."

"I was the only person at the matinee today. Nobody *ever* goes to the matinee on weekdays. I don't think anyone knows the theater is open during the week."

"Josh got pushed on the playground today. There are *never* any teachers on the playground to keep an eye on the kids."

It's all around you, every day. It's online and in the real world. Poor service. Unsafe conditions. Underutilized businesses.

Those are all indications of service or knowledge gaps.

Guess what?

You might be able to fill that service or knowledge gap.

That service or knowledge gap could be your *new job*.

Taking Action

When we encounter a problem, and it's irritating enough, we might complain about it.

Consider the first example above, the long wait at the post office. What happens when you have to wait twenty minutes to buy stamps?

You might ask to speak to a supervisor—or even the local postmaster—and blow off some steam.

"Why did I have to stand in line twenty minutes? You never have enough customer service windows open! It's such a waste of time. Why don't you have a window for simple purchases, like stamps? The lines would move so much faster. Why don't you hire more people?" Etc., etc., etc.

The supervisor or postmaster might be indifferent, or they might listen to you. However they respond, a few minutes later you'll be back out on the sidewalk. You might feel better for having blown off some steam—but you still don't have a job.

What if you had asked to speak to the supervisor or postmaster, and you kept your temper?

What if instead of complaining, you said something along the lines of "I notice when I come in here that you usually only have one or two windows open. You don't seem to have enough staff. Have you thought of hiring additional workers? Do you know if any job positions will be opening up here in the near future?"

The supervisor or postmaster might say no, they aren't doing hiring in the near future. They might say they'd like to hire, but there's no budget. In which case you hand them your card or your resume and *ask them to call you if and when there is a budget and an opening for a new worker.*

What if the supervisor says, they *are* planning to hire a couple of additional staff members? Wow. You had no idea. But now you know, because you took the time to talk calmly and productively with someone in charge. You have a bit of an edge now. You can research the job, see if you meet the qualifications, and whether it would suit you. You can start any training you need for the job. You can register for any necessary tests or exams.

This scenario illustrates the concept of *creating a job position for yourself*.

- **Notice where businesses have gaps.**
- **Calmly and politely point it out to someone in charge.**
- **Inquire about job openings.**
- **Offer your skills and expertise.**

This will work in pretty much any job field or industry. It will work in person, by phone, or online. Let's briefly review the other sample scenarios.

All Hands on Deck

The store that only has two registers open is like the post office where you have to wait twenty minutes for stamps. Ask to see the store manager. Tell her that you notice they rarely have more than two cash registers open. Suggest they hire additional cashiers. Mention your retail experience and give the manager your card and/or resume. Tell them you'd love to hear about cashier openings.

Take the Lead

What about the rude bank tellers at First National? If you have customer service and management experience, *ask the bank manager if he's ever considered hiring a customer service manager* to make sure the tellers are projecting a positive attitude to customers.

At many businesses, senior managers are locked away in back rooms buried under piles of paperwork. They don't always know—or even want to know—what's happening out front.

If you share your concerns and offer constructive solutions—the main solution being hiring *you*—you never know what that could lead to.

When trying to create leadership roles, emphasize the benefits (the win-wins) for everyone. E.g., if the bank hires a customer service manager and/or trainer, that would lead to improved service, improved customer satisfaction, greater customer loyalty, *and* a lot of paperwork and HR duties could be moved from the bank manager's desk to the customer service manager. That's a real selling point!

If You Build It ...

If you see a gas station—or any building—that looks like it's about to fall down, that appears unattractive or unsafe, and you have constructions skills, *ask to see someone in charge and offer to do some repairs*.

It's not just about earning a few bucks. *A few improvements and odd jobs could lead to a more permanent job for you.* And the repair projects are something else to put on your resume.

Best Face Forward

Do you have marketing, advertising, and/or PR skills? *Then you should be talking to managers at any underutilized business you've noticed.*

Consider the movie theater in the example above, the theater where almost no one attends the weekday matinees. *Someone* needs to get the word out about those matinees.

Talk with the theater manager. Better promotion of the matinees will increase attendance and mean more profits for the theater. Maybe more posters would help, or better posters, or better-placed posters, or a social media campaign online.

Offer your marking, advertising, and/or PR skills to the manager or owner. If they're interested, it might start as a short-term consulting job, just to help improve one aspect of their business, but *if you do an effective job and help increase the theater's profits, it could evolve into a full-time job.*

Have a Heart

How about the example where "little Josh" is being pushed around on the playground because there's inadequate supervision?

You could go to a PTA meeting and complain. You could leave an angry message on the superintendent's telephone.

Or you could go to the principal or superintendent, share your concerns about schoolyard safety, suggest the hiring of qualified schoolyard aids, and volunteer yourself for one of the positions.

Being a schoolyard aid will help the kids, add something to your resume, and if you have—or are willing and able to earn—the right credentials, could lead to even better jobs at the school.

Opportunity Knocks

Potential opportunity is everywhere. It's really a matter of perspective.

If you're looking for a job, and you see a place out there in your community where a business isn't living up to its potential, you can offer your skills and knowledge to bring that business up to its potential, and create a job for yourself.

This can be a difficult approach for shy job hunters, or job seekers who are feeling down about themselves.

But pick a time when you're feeling your best, take a deep breath, and give it a try.

You might get a few funny looks, and you might get a lot of rejection.

But when you speak up, somewhere along the line, someone in charge might listen to your thoughts about improving their business. They might like your credentials, and your initiative.

Your willingness to speak up might lead to your next job—and you might love it.

#17

HIRE YOURSELF!

You've searched high and low for a new job. You've been organized. You've figured out who you are. You've kept healthy. You've maintained a positive attitude. You've networked. You've written killer cover letters, resumes, and "thank you" notes. You've sent out applications and resumes. You've worked on projects and volunteered. You've taken classes to keep your skills current. You've even earned another certification and degree. You've joined professional organizations. You've identified service and knowledge gaps at community businesses, and offered your services to the managers and owners.

You've done everything right. Everything and more. But, still ... *No new job.*

When you can't land an existing job, and when you can't find a business that will create a new job for you, a possible next step is to *hire yourself*.

What does that mean?

You're out of work, you're on a tight budget. Hire yourself? Crazy talk!

This is another "out of the box" idea, but in this challenging job market, workers who can't get hired or rehired are becoming *self-employed* or *starting a small business*.

Could this be the right path for you?

Ask yourself the following questions:

- *Can you do something well that few others can do?*
- *Would you like to do that thing full time?*
- *Is there a need for that thing in your community (or on a larger scale)?*
- *Can you put the money together?*
- *Can you find (or do you already have) a space for your business?*
- *Are you willing to work long hours seven days a week?*
- *Are you willing and able to lose money the first few years?*
- *Do you have the creativity and problem-solving skills to deal with inevitable obstacles?*
- *Do you have the persistence to keep going in the face of inevitable set-backs?*
- *Do you already have clients who can help spread the word to attract additional clients?*
- *Do you have mentors who will share practical advice and insights to help jump-start, maintain, and grow your business?*
- *Do you have an emotional support system (friends and family) to encourage you during the tough times?*

The answers to all (or almost all) of these questions should be "Yes" before you proceed.

Reality Check

On television or in the movies, characters who are self-employed or run their own businesses are typically portrayed as having all sorts of free time on their hands.

This is because most television programs and films are driven by drama. Characters who can set their own schedules can be placed in a lot of dramatic situations—more than a secretary stuck at a desk for eight hours a day or a factory worker stuck at an assembly line!

So on TV and in the movies, entrepreneurial characters are rarely at work. They are at home, at their romantic interest's home, out-on-the-town, at a museum, at a sporting event, at an art gallery, on a sailboat, on horseback—they are pretty much anywhere but at their place of business. They always seem to have plenty of money, and any business problems that arise are solved quickly.

This portrayal of the entrepreneurial life *in no way reflects reality*.

The real deal?

- **Long Hours.** Whether you decide to write full-time, or become a freelance engineer, or run your own restaurant—whatever business you start—you will be working long, *long* hours. Your family and friends have to be OK with you essentially disappearing into your work for long stretches of time, at all hours of the day and night.

- **Demanding Schedules.** Yes, in some ways your schedule will be flexible. As "the boss" you can arrange your projects and meetings so that you can drop the kids at school and pick them up, so that you can meet your sister for lunch or your best friend for an evening jog. But for the most part you will be glued to your office, your computer, your restaurant, because it's *your* business. If you have clients in other states or countries, you will find yourself scheduling meetings and deadlines for odd hours to accommodate other time zones. Even if you have a few employees—or even a lot of employees—the whole endeavor is going to succeed or fail based on *your* work, *your* sweat, *your* commitment, *your* vision. Problems that arise will all roll up to you, because you're the chief decision-maker.

- **Money.** You will *always* be worried about money, especially the first few years. No matter how simple your operation is, there will be expenses and income. You have to record, track, reconcile, and report on all money coming in and flowing out. If you have employees, you have all the headaches of payroll. If you have suppliers, distributors, and contracts, your financial issues become even more complex. Not only is the money side of things time-consuming and complex, many times you won't have enough money. It generally takes at least three to five years for entrepreneurs and small businesses to start making a profit. If you haven't started to break even and see profits after a few years, you either need to fix your business model and marketing plans or quit.

With all that in mind, ask yourself the key questions again.

Do you do something few others can do? Will people want to pay for that service or product? Can you put in the time and effort? Will those close to you support you? Do you have or can you find a place for your business? Can you put together the money to finance this endeavor, whether through savings or loans or investors?

If you answered "Yes" to all or most of the initial questions, your next logical step is to create your business plan.

Business Plans

A business plan is your road map when you're self-employed or starting your own business.

The plan maps out the answers to many of the key questions above:

What will your business be? What products and services will you provide? What makes them unique or special? How and where will you provide them? Where will you get your supplies and materials? Who will your customers be? How will you reach customers? What type of employees and infrastructure will you need? How will you make money? What will your risks be? Will you need a lawyer? An accountant? Will you need licenses and permits? Will you need to incorporate? Will you need branding, logos, signs, a business name? Will you need to advertise? How much space will you need? How much will all this cost? What will capital and operating costs be? Where will the money come from? How much do you expect to earn? What will your taxes be? What will your net earnings be? When will you start to break even?

It's a lot to consider, and it can be tough to put together a business plan on your own.

- If you have the funds, you can hire someone to help you build your business plan.
- If not, you can reach out for non-profit assistance.
- If you're a business person, you might be able to do it yourself.

Obviously it's simpler for a freelance writer or artist to put together a business plan than it is for someone opening a landscaping service or someone opening a restaurant. But even the simplest self-employment endeavor should have some kind of realistic business plan in place.

Realistic is the key word. Take the time to think through *everything* that you'll be taking on as a self-employed person or business owner.

Let's examine a very simple scenario: the self-employed writer.

- Even a freelance writer has a lot to contend with. On the surface it *seems* simple. All a writer needs is a computer, an internet connection, some paper, and a little imagination. Right? Well … it's a bit more complicated.

- Like any self-employed person, writers need to factor in things like paying self-employment tax. Depending on how much a writer earns and where he earns it, he might actually need an accountant, unless he knows how to do his own bookkeeping.

- There are expected costs to contend with, like research and travel and equipment expenses. And then there are those unexpected expenses. Laptops break, printers and scanners break, and flash drives and software don't always come cheap.

- Legal issues like copyright infringement can arise—so consulting a lawyer might be necessary from time-to-time.

- And where are the writer's clients coming from? Do they drop out of the sky? (Would that it were so!) Writers need to do some sort of advertising and promotion, which can be costly. And it's often advantageous for them join professional groups which require annual fees or dues.

That's just scratching the surface of all that's involved in being self-employed.

And that's the *simplest* self-employed scenario—a a writer operating out of her house with zero employees and low overhead.

Someone who wants to open a restaurant, or day-care center, or art gallery, is looking at a *much* more complicated business plan that will involve licenses, lawyers, real estate, and at least a couple of employees.

If you've read this far, and you're still intrigued by self-employment, then good for you. You very well might be someone who will thrive in a self-employed environment.

Go for it. Start researching and putting together your business plan.

Making the Vision Real

Once your realistic and detailed business plan is in place, your next steps are to make the vision a reality.

You gather the funding—if you can.

You secure your space and hire your experts and—if applicable—start hiring your employees and buying your materials and equipment.

You establish your distribution channels.

You secure your licenses and permits. You pass safety inspections.

You begin producing your goods and services.

Now you need buyers, customers, or clients.

So you launch your marketing plan. You get the word out. You enlist others who already know how amazing you are, and they help spread the word. You use printed material, radio or TV (if you can afford it), websites, and social media, as well as good old-fashioned word-of-mouth.

It's a long process, a lot of work, and sometimes it breaks your heart. Sometimes you create the product, you arrange the service, you put out the word—but nobody buys your service or product. Or somebody buys your service or product—but not enough to keep you afloat in the long run.

Have you read this far? Are you still intrigued by the thought of self-employment?

Then ask those questions. Develop a business plan. Make your vision a reality.

And see where it takes you.

#18

AVOID KOOKY STUNTS

Sometimes, especially if you've been out-of-work for more than six months, if your bank account is running low, and the job offers still aren't coming in, you might be tempted to start thinking *waaaaay* outside of the box to land a job.

In the wee small hours of the night, as you're trying to figure out how to make the next mortgage payment, crazy ideas might come to you. Crazy stunts that might get you hired.

Here's the thing. At the end of the day, crazy stunts are pretty much crazy. And desperate. And that's *not* how you want to be viewed in the job-hunting arena.

- *Should you make a sandwich board with a pithy "Hire Me!" message scrawled across it, and wear it while you walk up and down Main Street?*
- *Should you draw a cartoon character on your resume?*
- *Print your resumes on neon-pink paper?*
- *List your name as "Fred Flintstone" or "Betty Rubble" on job applications?*
- *Should you dress in a dramatic or bizarre way for job interviews?*
- *Dye your hair bright green?*

- *Skateboard into the building and do your half-pipe routine in the lobby?*

- *Behave like a mime when meeting a prospective employer for the first time?*

- *Crump your way into the interview room?*

- *Answer interview questions by singing lyrics to a relevant U2 or Faith Hill song?*

- *Answer interview questions in a dead language (like Latin or Sumerian)?*

- *Juggle during the interview?*

- *Announce that you are the reincarnation of Joan of Arc?*

- *Do your best Richard Nixon impression, saying "I am not a crooook," when the interview concludes?*

The answer to all of these questions—*all* of them—should be *no*. Emphatically no.

And yes, these are rather silly examples. But they're ridiculous to make a point.

Whatever you consider doing to grab the attention of the recruiters or interviewers, think about this: *You* are seeing the unusual move as a way to capture their attention. But how will *they* see it? Will it simply seem awkward and/or bizarre to them?

Probably.

As always, the exception to this mandate is if you are an artist or entertainer. If you work in a creative field, there might be someone at the prospective employer's organization that will be impressed by your bright green hair, your miming, or your half-pipe routine, who will think that answering boring old interview questions with Faith Hill lyrics is a stroke of genius worthy of making you the VP of Public Relations on the spot.

Maybe. Possibly. It depends on the organization, and on the position you're applying for.

But typically it's not worth the chance.

Even at creative organizations, there tend to be layers of (usually) conservative recruiters and HR staff members that you need to impress before you get to meet the managers and team members you'd be working with day-to-day.

Recruiters and HR staff members are flooded with applications. *They are just looking for reasons to kick applications and resumes to the curb*, to winnow the towering piles of paper on their desks, and thin out the trillion messages in their overcrowded email in-boxes. Don't give them a reason to reject you.

If you work in a creative field, you will likely be asked to provide a sample of your work. Head shots and demo videos for actors, musicians, and other performers. Portfolios for artists, designers, photographers, and writers. *That's* where you should let your creativity shine. Not by pulling quirky or kooky stunts.

It's rough, looking for work in this job market. Only those who have been through it get it.

So you lie there as you fall asleep, thinking of kooky ways to get employers' attention.

Go ahead and brainstorm about printing your business cards on slices of Swiss cheese, or projecting your resume into the sky like the Bat Signal.

Brainstorming is harmless. And it releases stress.

But when you wake up the next day, let the kooky ideas go.

#19

NEVER LET THEM SEE YOU SWEAT

It's rather cruel but it's human nature—people want to hire the candidate who seems so competent and successful, so calm and so collected, *that they don't seem to need the job.*

What about the highly qualified applicant who's beginning to seem desperate?

One whiff of that desperation, and employers tend to drop that candidate like a hot potato.

It's not your fault if you feel desperate. Months out of work, years, even. That struggle to make ends meet. The psychological toll and emotional toll that long-term unemployment can take. Long-term job-hunting is a rough ride. One of the roughest rides anyone can endure.

Vent to friends and family. Lean on them for support.

But once you hit that job interview, you *have* to pull it together.

To paraphrase the old deodorant commercial: Never, never, *never* let potential employers or professional peers see you sweat.

Special tips for the anxious job-hunter.

- **Look and feel your best when you head to a job interview.** Practice your interview questions with someone you trust. Exercise a couple of hours before the meeting—exercise makes us feel better about ourselves, even if it's a few stretches or a brief walk. Eat a little something (healthy and light) so your stomach's not growling. Be perfectly groomed, with fresh breath, and no scent or light scent (don't douse yourself in perfume or cologne!). If you tend to perspire, hit the rest room right before the meeting to dab. Wear a blazer (summer-weight or heavy depending upon the season) and sweat shields if needed.

- **Mentally repeat positive mantras. Tell yourself the truth—that you're a winner.** Only a winner can keep going, keep trying, keep picking themselves up again and again. Take deep breaths. Tell yourself that you're a winner. This is the type of positive self-talk you need playing in your head like a soundtrack, not only before an interview but also before a meeting with any professional peers or prospective job leads.

- **Smile. Smile like you mean it.** When you smile, it has a real effect on your well-being, as well as the way others perceive you.

- **Tell yourself "I don't really need this job."** This is a little bit of self-hypnosis that can slow your pulse and calm your breathing. Maybe you do need this job. Maybe your whole life depends on it. But during an interview or at any professional gathering where peers and potential employers can observe you, tell yourself you *don't* need it. Take a deep breath. Mentally repeat "I don't need this job" several times. Repeat it during the meeting as necessary. Sure, it sounds like a cool job. It would be cool to have it. But you don't *need* it. This is what you need to believe so you can relax during the interview, even enjoy it, and really pay attention, instead of stressing out and blowing your chances.

- **Even if you're anxious about money, never discuss salary during the first interview** unless the interviewer raises the issue. If you have financial troubles, and you raise the issue, the interviewer will probably see or sense your nerves. Not a good impression to make.

- **Never ask interviewers "When will you make a decision?"** If they're interested in you, they'll share the decision timeframe at the end of the interview or soon after. It can take nerves of steel, but tough it out. Do not ask this question. Seeming like you're not anxious can increase your bargaining position. Seeming anxious hurts your bargaining position and can even sabotage the job offer.

- **Never complain or sound angry.** No matter how friendly they are during the interview, potential employers are not our moms, spouses, or best friends. However low you are feeling, however anxious, and however friendly and down-to-earth the interviewers seem, *never* voice your complaints to them or share sad-sack stories. Don't tell them you're two months behind on your mortgage. Don't tell them your wife might leave you. Don't tell them you think life is unfair and that incompetent employees and managers should be sent on a one-way rocket trip to the moon. Similarly, even if you're feeling (understandably) bitter these days, don't let an edge of anger creep into your voice. Anger is a deal-breaker. No one wants to hire an angry person. When you're at an interview or any gathering of your professional peers, be positive. Stay focused on the job, your qualifications, and why you're a great match for the jobs you're pursuing.

- **Maintain the body language of a winner.** During interviews and in all professional settings, sit up straight, leaning slightly back in the chair to indicate ease, leaning slightly forward from time to time to indicate interest in what an interviewer is saying. Maintain eye contact, including everyone on the interview panel. Don't fold your arms or put your hands in your pockets. Keep your hands open, a gesture indicating honesty and even benevolence.

- **Keep smiling.** (See bullet 3 above.) Some candidates start out smiling, but they forget to smile as the interview or meeting progresses.

- **Don't look thrown.** Practice a calmly smiling poker face. Whatever questions or disappointments get thrown at you, keep that calm expression. You will be thrown from time-to-time—just don't look it.

- **Express disappointment if you're told you didn't get a job, but don't fall apart.** It's a terrible moment when you learn you're not getting the job, especially if you really, really wanted and/or needed it. You will feel a sinking sensation in the pit of your stomach, and visions of delinquent bills will float in front of your eyes. But don't fall apart now. You can do that later if you need to. Right now, give the interviewer a rueful smile and hearty handshake. You're disappointed, but you're a winner, so you know there will be other opportunities for you. Say "I'm sorry to hear that. I thought I'd be a great fit. If you think of another role where I might help the company, I'd love to hear from you." See? You're gracious in defeat. That will make a positive impression. Since you made it to the interview stage, you know they liked your credentials. If another opening comes up, they're likely to consider you again based on your positive attitude.

- **Express quiet satisfaction if you do get the job.** It's a wonderful moment when you hear you got the job—especially if you've been job hunting for a long time. But don't lose your cool now and start high-fiving everyone in the room or pumping your fist like you just threw a touchdown! Maintain your dignity. It's fine to look pleased. Give a hearty handshake to the interviewers. Tell them you're happy to hear they want to hire you. Ask simply "What are the next steps?" and they'll give you timeframes and tell you about paperwork you'll have to sign and orientations you'll have to attend. Be pleased but maintain that winner attitude. *Let them worry that if they don't offer a solid salary and benefits package, they might lose you.* If you are running around the room shouting "Finally! I *finally* got a job!" there goes your negotiating power!!

It's OK to be anxious. It's normal, understandable, excusable—all of the above. Share your emotions with those closest to you.

But put on your positive game face in all job-hunting situations. That's how you're going to finally land that new job.

#20

CELEBRATE YOUR VICTORY

When that day comes, when you close the deal and start a new job, whether you've been hired by someone else, or have launched your own business, you need to *celebrate*.

You need to notify, and thank, everyone who helped you along the long and bumpy road of job searching.

The former boss who wrote you a reference.

The former coworker whose timely tip put you onto this job.

The print shop team who showed you how to print your cover letters.

The coffee shop team who caffeinated you every morning.

Your kids, who were quiet (mostly quiet) and left you alone (mostly alone) while you wrote resumes and searched online job sites.

Your mother, who called you every evening and told you how special you are, no matter how the day's job search went.

Your spouse, who let you rant about the incompetence of HR departments on a daily basis, and didn't divorce you.

And so many more. No one finds a job completely on their own. There are at least a few people you need to thank, if you think about it.

And you might be surprised by how happy they will be to hear your good news. They might sound almost as happy about your new job as you do!

A simple verbal "thank you". A handwritten note. A small denomination gift card ($5 or $10). Flowers. A plant. Drinks and dinner. These are all ways to thank people who helped you, ways to invite them to join you in celebrating. The elaborateness of your "thank you" will depend on how well you know someone and how much they helped you.

Congratulations, job hunter! You did it. Bask in the joy, share the joy.

And once you're on your feet again, once you're settled into your new job, think about all the people who are still looking for jobs.

If you can encourage someone you know in that situation, write them a reference, give them a bit of advice, direct them toward a company you know is hiring—whatever you can do to help them will be a beautiful "pay it forward".

Congratulations again, job hunter.

May your new job be everything you hoped it would be!

RESOURCES

RESUME SAMPLE

Your resume will be unique to you and your industry, but it should follow some simple rules:

- **Be concise.** Short, succinct sentences and phrases, bullet points, and plenty of white space.

- **Be clear.** Correct spelling and grammar, and concrete statistics and details.

- **Be engaging.** Include your highlights—top skills and accomplishments. Use active verbs.

SAMPLE

ALONDRA X. GUPTA, M.A.

123 Barn Street, Deer Crossing, ME 03908 | (207) 555-5555 | alondra.x.gupta@email.com

DEVELOPMENT MANAGER

Human development professional who drives results by designing and executing training for employees at all levels across industries. Self-starter and team-player who reduces costs and increases productivity. Project Management and Six Sigma Certification. Master's degree in Management. Fluent in Spanish.

PROFESSIONAL EXPERIENCE

ABC GREETING CARDS   Deer Crossing, ME   04/2010 – Present
TRAINING MANAGER
Reduce training costs by $900K+ by teaming with the business unit leaders to identify skill gaps and to design and deliver training for all levels of employees.

- Saved $700K by developing a training program to improve rate of production.
- Reduced new employee travel expenses by 100% by rolling out online training modules.
- Generated $1M per annum in cost savings by streamlining and centralizing client training.

ETHAN UNIVERSITY   Bangor, ME   07/2001 – 02/2010
TRAINING MANAGER
Rolled out training programs that increased quality and efficiency across academic programs.

- Managed all campus training, from design to delivery to evaluation. Cost savings: $2M.
- Served as liaison between faculty and students regarding competing development requirements.
- Implemented standardized proctor training and protocols, reducing student complaints by 73%.

INTERNAL REVENUE SERVICES   Bangor, ME   08/1998 – 06/2001
TRAINING & DEVELOPMENT ASSOCIATE
Created and delivered financial protocol training for 150 IRS agents across Maine.

- Decreased rework by 55% by standardizing audit practices via centralized development.
- Won *Employee of the Month* in July 2000 for saving $1.5M via paperless training initiative.

EDUCATION

Master of Arts, Management, *Bowdoin College*   1998
Bachelor of Arts, English, *Bowdoin College*   1996

TRAINING CERTIFICATION

- *A.C.T.I.V.E. Leadership*
- *Project Management (PMP)*
- *Six Sigma*

USEFUL WEBSITES

You might find the following websites to be useful during your job search.

US Department of Labor Unemployment Insurance (UI) Information:

http://www.dol.gov/dol/topic/unemployment-insurance/

Free DiSC Personality Test to Help You Identify Possible Career Paths:

http://discpersonalitytesting.com/free-disc-test/

Simply Hired Job Search—Receive Email Updates About Jobs You Might Like:

http://www.simplyhired.com/

IRS Small Business & Self-Employment Tax Information:

http://www.irs.gov/Businesses/Small-Businesses-&-Self-Employed

National Institute of Mental Health (NIMH)—Free Publications:

http://www.nimh.nih.gov/health/publications/index.shtml

(The author is not compensated or employed by any of these sites.)

AUTHOR INFORMATION

Leslie Le Mon was raised in Germany and New England, and has lived in Los Angeles since 1992. She is an author, photographer, and manager. Leslie has been writing client resumes and coaching job hunters for almost fifteen years. She has been a hiring manager at corporate, non-profit, and academic organizations. Leslie is deeply indebted to career mentors like Cathy, Margaret, Rod, Nancy, Azar, Chris, Joanne, Mary, and Alicia—thank you for the coaching in years past.

Email: les.lemon.author@gmail.com

Twitter: @leslemonauthor

Website: www.leslielemonauthor.com

Search for Leslie's other fiction and non-fiction books at

Amazon.com

and

BarnesandNoble.com

and

Other fine booksellers

COPYRIGHT INFORMATION

This book and its contents, including text, graphics, and the cover design, are copyrighted by Leslie Le Mon, 2014.

Do not reproduce or reprint any content without the permission of the author.

Please direct inquiries to les.lemon.author@gmail.com.

www.ingramcontent.com/pod-product-compliance
Lightning Source LLC
Chambersburg PA
CBHW051710170526
45167CB00002B/617